WHAT PEOPLE ARE SAYING ABOUT
AFTER THE HONEYMOON . . .

"Every couple must pick up this fun and inspiring devotional book that mirrors pastor Rod Loy's passion to empower marriages. If you're searching to grow in your spirit along with your spouse, I wholeheartedly encourage you to check out this gem of a book."

—Gary Smalley, bestselling author and speaker, Colorado Springs, CO

"The excitement of marriage surpasses the wedding day when you make the daily decision to enjoy life together. *After the Honeymoon* will put some zest into your marriage by focusing on timeless wisdom that covers physical to spiritual needs and everything in between to help you build a God-honoring and joyful marriage."

—Ted Cunningham, pastor, Woodland Hills Family Church, Branson, MO, Author of *The Power of Home*

"Wow! What an awesome book—straightforward, challenging, and fun! One of the things I love most is seeing couples with healthy marriages, but in our culture, thriving marriages aren't the norm. I'm so excited to suggest this practical book, *After the Honeymoon*, to people who want their marriage to grow stronger and deeper. Thank you, Rod. You nailed it!"

—Joe Cyr, lead pastor, Life Church, Manchester, NH

"Getting married is the easy part. Knowing what to do when you wake up as Mr. and Mrs. takes some intentional work. Rod Loy leverages his passion for his son, Tyler, to enjoy a life-giving marriage and his pastoral heart to see people thrive in God-honoring lives into this powerful tool. No newlyweds should be without it. *After the Honeymoon* provides clear and practical biblical guidance for marriage in a fun and irresistible manner that will leave an eternal mark on every couple."

—Jason M. Karampatsos, PhD, LCPC, NCC, marriage counselor and cofounder of City of Refuge Counseling Network

"*After the Honeymoon* will help any married (or soon to be married) couple assess many important aspects of their relationship and make wise decisions to move forward. I highly recommend that spouses walk together through this incredible resource."

—Nathan Kollar, pastor, Clarity, Los Angeles, CA

"Heidi and I wish there had been a book like this when we started our marriage! This book is unique because it comes from a father's heart for his son and daughter-in-law. This isn't someone spouting off random marriage advice. It's a family discussion of love, intimacy, and marriage, and we get to sit in and listen."

—Randy Jumper, young adult pastor, First Assembly of God, North Little Rock, AR

"As a marriage and family therapist, I often help young couples adjust their expectations early in marriage. In *After the Honeymoon*, Rod Loy addresses many of the fundamental struggles discovered by newlyweds. This scripturally based, practical approach to an important marital season is both clinically sound and thoroughly applicable."

—Dr. Ryan Darrow, lead pastor, Overland Park First Assembly of God, Overland Park, KS, marriage and family therapist

"In a day and age where marriage is increasingly devalued, Rod Loy addresses foundational truths that will strengthen couples who are newly married (and those who have been married a while). This book needs to be read and reread by every newlywed couple in order to establish stability and health early on in the marriage."

—Aaron Hlavin, lead pastor, Freedom Christian, Sterling Heights, MI

"The wisdom and honor Pastor Rod imparts transcends the beginning of a marriage. These are timeless truths that cultivate a healthy life-long commitment, and apply to every age and season of each unique marriage. The spiritual and physical union of two individuals becoming one in Christ is a sacred trust that must be tended to and invested for the rest of life. Applying these powerful principles will strengthen your marital union and leave a legacy to be passed on for generations to come."

—Jennifer McAfee, lead pastor, Villages Community, Fort Worth, TX

"Anything that comes from Rod Loy's deep well of wisdom is bound to be a lasting treasure in my library. Like everything else Rod offers, you will find this book to be a great resource to serve the church for generations. Full of practical wisdom, humor, and vulnerability, his writing offers the insights he gave to his son Tyler and daughter-in-law, Emilie. Any couple who reads it will be better for it."

—Mike Burnette, lead pastor, LifePoint Church, Clarksville, TN

"The habits we implement in our daily routines set the direction for our lives. The same can be said of our marriages. We need to begin our marriages with good habits. This book is uniquely written to help young couples form enduring habits to build a strong and healthy marriage. So whether you are newlyweds or a seasoned married couple, these ninety days of readings will inspire, encourage, and help you build a marriage that thrives."

—Dr. Andrew Templeton, lead pastor, First Assembly of God, Sweetwater, TN

AFTER THE HONEYMOON

90 Days to a Thriving Marriage

ROD LOY

Published by Influence Resources
1445 N. Boonville Ave.
Springfield, Missouri 65802

Cover design by Sheepish Design www.sheepishdesign.org
Interior formatting by Anne McLaughlin, Blue Lake Design, Dickinson, Texas

ISBN: 978-1-62912-189-5

18 17 16 15 • 1 2 3 4
Printed in the United States of America

This book is dedicated to my wife, Cindy, and our two sons, Tyler and Parker.

With laughter, joy, and a few tears, Cindy and I have learned these lessons together. I look forward to many more years of learning!

It was Tyler and Emilie's wedding that inspired me to write these words of advice. Watching them grow closer to God and to each other is a source of great joy.

Just before this book went to press, my younger son, Parker, got engaged. He and Meredith will be married in 2016. I'm glad these words are already written for them!

Thank you all for filling my life with meaningful memories and abundant joy. I love you and I'm proud of you!

CONTENTS

A LETTER FROM ROD . . .

Oops! The book you are holding in your hand is an "accident." Before you put it down, let me explain . . .

I love being a dad! Watching my sons Tyler and Parker grow in maturity has been one of life's greatest joys. A new phase began for all of us last year when Tyler met and fell in love with Emilie Bullock. He proposed, and Emilie accepted.

As Tyler and Emilie's wedding date approached, I wanted to pass along important lessons and key principles my wife, Cindy, and I have learned during our twenty-seven-year marriage. No marriage is perfect, but ours has been pretty wonderful. Each morning I wrote a thought for that day and posted it on Facebook.

My motive for writing was simple: I desperately wanted Tyler and Emilie to have a thrilling, healthy, lifelong marriage. I wanted to help them anticipate challenges, determine their responses in advance, and build their relationship on solid biblical principles.

What happened next surprised me. People started reposting and sharing my daily updates. I hadn't written to appeal to the masses or sell a product, but requests for the lessons in book form filled my in-box, so I compiled them into this "accidental" book.

I had to depersonalize some of the material, but the truths I hoped to communicate have remained the same. One of the things I'm most excited about is that this book contains much more than merely what I know about marriage. I'm passing along what I've learned (from personal example as well as from teaching) from a vast number of sources dear to Tyler, Emilie, Cindy, and me, including: Tyler's grandmother, Emilie's grandparents, Jim and Betty Rodgers, Dorothy Murray, Paul and Becky Roden, Greg Beggs, Scott Hanson, Russell and Laverne Edwards, David and Beth Grant, Glenn and Reta Russell, Patrick and Suzi Lander, and countless others. Thanks to such people, Cindy and I have learned how to grow as a couple, how to go through suffering together, how to have fun in spite of life's stormy circumstances, and all sorts of other ways to live life to the fullest.

I pray that you and your new spouse will be helped and encouraged by our mistakes, failures, and successes as you work your way through these pages. Read one thought each day for the next ninety days. Discuss the principle with your spouse.

Answer the question or do the exercise together. The investment you are about to make will yield a lifetime of rewards!

Putting together a great wedding takes time, money, thought, creativity, and more than a little patience! Creating a great marriage takes time, work, prayer, and intentional focus. Now that your wedding is over . . . make your marriage great!

Rod Loy

P. S. Even if you've been married a while, these principles will still work for you. Let the next ninety days rekindle and strengthen your marriage!

ONE

IMPERFECTLY EVER AFTER

No matter how hard you hope and try,
no marriage will be perfect.

For the last several months (if not years), your focus has been on your wedding. You worried, of course, because you wanted everything to be perfect: Would it rain? Would the flower girls cry? Would someone trip or faint? Would anyone throw up? Would the cake be perfect? Would families fight?

Yet in spite of your combined efforts, I'm guessing something went wrong. I've presided at more than a hundred weddings, and something unplanned has threatened to complicate every one of them, despite the bride's best-laid plans. It just happens.

Keep that in mind as you now shift your focus from your *wedding* to your *marriage*. After all that stressing and planning, the wedding is now but a moment in your past, captured in pictures. Your marriage, however, is ongoing and forever. The effort you put into planning your wedding is just a fraction what will be needed from now on. If something went wrong at the wedding, you were surrounded by family, attendants, and other friends who hurried to solve the problem. From now on, you and your spouse are primarily responsible to work out the imperfections in life and marriage . . . and those imperfections will pop up with great regularity.

A healthy marriage is equal parts friendship, romantic love, and partnership. All three areas require intentional attention to remain strong. None of them develop automatically. So work on your friendship and nurture your romantic love; negotiate, compromise, and communicate as you forge a strong partnership. And enjoy your wonderful, beautiful, imperfect marriage happily ever after!

THOUGHT FOR THE DAY

"Many waters cannot quench love; rivers cannot sweep it away. If one were to give all the wealth of one's house for love, it would be utterly scorned" (Song of Songs 8:7).

TODAY'S ACTIVITY

Independently list what you feel will be your three biggest challenges during your first year of marriage. Then get together, share your lists with one another, and start brainstorming how you will respond.

Among the most beautiful elements of marriage is love that covers over a multitude of imperfections. Offer grace joyously.

@NathanKollar

TWO

NOT ALL GOOD THINGS MUST COME TO AN END

Make your honeymoon last forever.

I suspect you've recently had certain people pull you aside and say things like: "Enjoy the honeymoon. It doesn't last long." "(S)He won't be the same person as when you were dating." "Now, reality sets in."

Those people have one thing in common: they're all *wrong*! Don't listen to people who say such negative, discouraging things. Here's the great truth—*you* get to choose how long the honeymoon lasts. *You* get to choose your reality, not some disgruntled person who chose the wrong approach. Don't let people who are miserable in their marriage speak misery into yours.

Do you want to make the honeymoon last forever? Here are a few ideas to get you started:

Every morning thank God for your spouse. It will remind you how blessed you are and make it more difficult to be critical.

Say "I love you" every time you walk out the door and every time you end a call.

Sneak a kiss in the elevator.

Hold hands when you walk. (It's okay. Married couples are still allowed.)

Secretly set aside money to buy a special gift. It doesn't have to be big, just something meaningful.

You get the idea. Add to the list as you wish. Most importantly, regularly spend time with other happily married couples who are obviously still in love. Trust me, they're out there!

Cindy and I have been married twenty-seven years. I would like to say we're as happy as we were twenty-seven years ago, but the truth is . . . we're happier!

THOUGHT FOR THE DAY

"Be on your guard; stand firm in the faith; be courageous; be strong. Do everything in love" (1 Corinthians 16:13–14).

TODAY'S ACTIVITY

Pull out photos and mementos from your honeymoon as you recall the good times you had. Discuss how you can keep your love fresh and extend the honeymoon phase forever. Determine the things you liked best about the honeymoon (setting, activities, solitude together etc.,). Then get out your planning calendars for the next year and set aside some dates at intermittent intervals to schedule similar experiences.

The best choices cultivate the best marriage. #uGET2choose #1Cor16v14
@Jennifer_McAfee

THREE

WHAT ARE *YOU* LOOKING AT?

Focus on and celebrate the positive aspects of your spouse.

Think back to standing at the altar and saying your vows to that person who couldn't seem more right for you. Didn't (s)he look great? You probably felt like the luckiest person in the world because, at the time, all you could see were the person's best traits.

However, as time passes you are likely to discover other aspects of that person that aren't quite as desirable. At that point, if couples begin to dwell on negatives, they can set off on a course that tends to get rocky very quickly. It is far better to determine to always acknowledge and celebrate the positive characteristics of your spouse.

I like how Pastor Craig Groeschel puts it:

Think about the difference between two birds: a vulture and a humming-bird. Vultures soar high in the sky looking and searching . . . until they find lifeless, rotting roadkill. Contrast the vulture to the tiny hummingbird. With wings flapping twenty beats a second, what does this small bird find? Not dead things and disgusting rancid meat, but instead, sweet, life-giving nectar. Daily, each bird finds what he is looking for. The same is true for you.[1]

The principle is true not just for marriage, but for all areas of life: Look for the best and you will find it; look for something to criticize and that's what you will find. Have some fun searching for the best in your spouse, because you find what you seek. It's what brought you together, and it's what will keep you together.

---

1   Craig Groeschel, *Soul Detox* (Grand Rapids: Zondervan, 2013), 50.

THOUGHT FOR THE DAY

"The eye is the lamp of the body. If your eyes are healthy, your whole body will be full of light" (Matthew 6:22).

TODAY'S ACTIVITY

Make a list of the things you like best about your spouse. Share your lists with one another and then determine a fun way to celebrate so many positive things as you begin your marriage. (I will have you repeat this exercise several times throughout the book to help you make this a regular habit.)

Remember always to see the best in one another. If you need help, ask Jesus. He sees the best in you; aren't you glad?
@pastorjoecyr

FOUR

THE OBJECT OF CHANGE

Strive to change yourself, not your spouse.

Suppose you buy a car, sign the papers, and drive it home. You put a lot of miles on it that first weekend, but then you show up at the dealer's the next week and explain that you decided you would rather have the larger engine . . . or the red model instead of the blue . . . or an upgrade to the leather interior. How do you think the salesperson would respond?

You would soon discover that a car sale is a "done deal." How much more so is a marriage license! When you promised "to take this (wo)man," the understanding was that the person comes "as is." Yet before long it becomes tempting to point out things your spouse needs to change, and those things can quickly become a lengthy list! Unfortunately, that list usually creates more dissension than improvement.

Resist the impulse to change your spouse. Instead, make it your goal to change *yourself*—to become and do whatever it takes to enable your spouse to fulfill what God created him or her to be. That's your quest. Ask yourself every day, "What can I do or say to help her excel today?" "What can I change in myself that will bring out the very best in him?"

When you determine to alter the object of change from your spouse to yourself, it's amazing how God molds and shapes you as a couple. Few things will bring you closer together than helping one another realize your God-given purpose.

THOUGHT FOR THE DAY

"We urge you, brothers and sisters, warn those who are idle and disruptive, encourage the disheartened, help the weak, be patient with everyone. Make sure that nobody pays back wrong for wrong, but always strive to do what is good for each other and for everyone else" (1 Thessalonians 5:14–15).

TODAY'S ACTIVITY

This one's for you as individuals: prayerfully ponder what change(s) you might make in yourself that would make your spouse a better person. Then give some thought as to how to begin making that change.

Don't look to make changes in your spouse, rather take personal responsibility for your words and actions. Change is purposeful.
@ryandarrow

FIVE

NOTHING TO HIDE

Marriage enables you to be fully known and still fully loved.

When I was a kid, I wore thick glasses. One summer I discovered that if I held my glasses close enough to dry brush or a piece of paper, I could focus the sun's rays through the lens and start a fire, just like with a magnifying glass. I started a lot of fires with those glasses.

Marriage is like a magnifying glass. The close relational focus between spouses intensifies and magnifies, and before long it may create some heat!

As a kid, I was a misfit. (The thick glasses might have given you a clue.) I experienced the pain of ridicule and rejection, but I didn't want the other kids to know how much it hurt so I became quite clever at hiding my true feelings. But when I got married, Cindy soon saw through my façade. At first I feared rejection, even from my wife. But Cindy loved and accepted me in spite of my insecurities. With her help, I learned to deal with them, rather than just pretend they didn't exist.

It was refreshing and freeing to come out of hiding. I'm still not completely free of my insecurities, but my authentic, loving relationship with Cindy opened the door for authentic relationships with others. I'm a better person because of marriage's magnifying glass!

Don't even try to hide your insecurities and fears. Your spouse sees you night and day, and at your most vulnerable times. As hard as you might try, everything hidden will be revealed. Instead, discover the joy of true intimacy—being fully known and fully loved.

THOUGHT FOR THE DAY

"[Love] always protects, always trusts, always hopes, always perseveres" (1 Corinthians 13:7).

TODAY'S ACTIVITY

Muster your courage and share one (or more) of your still-secret fears with your spouse, with the understanding that (s)he will be nothing but supportive in response.

Intimacy starts with each spouse committing to open and honest communication. Don't let insecurity prevent intimacy.
@randyjumper

SIX

DIVVY UP THE DUTIES

Learn to do what needs to be done
and equally divide dreaded chores.

When I got married, I was a typical guy. I had never done my own laundry. (I couldn't tell the washer from the dryer!) I didn't know how to cook—anything. I didn't know the right way to fold towels. I had never operated an iron. My mother had taken very good care of me for most of my life.

It didn't take long to learn . . . Cindy is not my Momma. Cindy loves to do nice things for me. And for the record, she's a good cook and knows how to do laundry. But that doesn't mean it's her "job" to take care of my every need, even when I try to plead incompetence. That would make her a slave, not a wife.

So I had some catching up to do. As it turns out, washers, dryers, irons, and most other appliances come with instruction manuals, but it's a lot more fun to learn from someone who already knows what (s)he's doing! Today if Cindy isn't around for some reason, I still fumble around in the kitchen and laundry room, but I can take care of myself . . . just a few of the lessons learned during my marriage so far.

You and your spouse are marriage *partners*, so divide household responsibilities equitably. It doesn't matter what other people do; choose what works for you. If the husband is the better cook and enjoys the kitchen, let him be the chef. If the wife enjoys exercise and outdoors, let her mow the lawn. When it comes to the chores that no one truly enjoys (vacuuming, cleaning toilets, etc.), either take turns or come to an agreement of "I'll do this if you'll do that." Then, when the work is done, be sure to get together and do something you both enjoy.

THOUGHT FOR THE DAY

"Whatever you do, work at it with all your heart, as working for the Lord, not for human masters" (Colossians 3:23).

TODAY'S ACTIVITY

If you haven't done so, sit down with your spouse and discuss your division of work concerning chores around the house. Does one of you feel you are doing more than your share? Are certain chores being ignored? How can you make your "chores" more fun? Work out a plan for the next week, and then regularly reevaluate and adjust if you need to.

It's a life lesson for sure, but healthy marriages learn and understand the value of sharing life and shared living.
@MikeBurnette

SEVEN

TRY DATING A
MARRIED PERSON

Just because you're married
doesn't mean you should stop dating.

I never cease to be amazed at how madly passionate some dating couples are about each other, and then they get married and barely speak to each other. They settle back into their previous demanding lifestyles and let the needs of their spouse remain unattended.

It's important to maintain an active dating life even now that you're married—*especially* now that you're married. It doesn't have to be expensive or overly time consuming, but you need to make time for one another. And it needs to remain *fun*.

Try this: Take turns picking something to do together—something you personally enjoy and think your spouse needs to experience. One of my recent choices was four-wheeling, and Cindy went home covered with mud! It was a great day. But she got even. When it was her turn, she picked a facial and a pedicure at a day spa. I was covered with who knows what, and more than a little embarrassed. But both experiences brought us closer as a couple, and we still laugh about both days!

Hey, you found (or made) time for one another while you were dating, didn't you? So keep it up! You have no greater priority right now than to ensure the strength of your new marriage. You will never regret the time you spend with one another in the early months of your relationship.

THOUGHT FOR THE DAY

"May the righteous be glad and rejoice before God; may they be happy and joyful" (Psalm 68:3).

TODAY'S ACTIVITY

You know what's coming, don't you? It's similar to the instructions on the back of your shampoo bottle: "Date. Enjoy. Repeat." Get out there and do something together . . . soon. If you need some suggestions, look through the "90 Dates for $10 or Less" section in the back of this book.

If you are married and want to be joyful when you are old, let "I Do" be the beginning of your best date yet.
@RachelLBRoss

EIGHT

THE MISSING PIECE

Having fun is not a sin.

When my parents were growing up, the church had a basic philosophy: "If it's fun, it must be sin." Included in that "sin" category were roller-skating, going to movies, playing pool, swimming, and other similar activities.

Some people still equate fun with sin, but they must be reading a different Bible than mine. My Bible speaks of cheerful hearts, laughter, dancing, and shouting and leaping for joy! If that's not fun, what is?

When it comes to establishing a healthy marriage, *not* having fun together should be a sin! Life is tough, the challenges are serious, the frustrations are many, and we all need a level of spiritual maturity to deal with everything. But that should never stop you from just having fun every now and then.

My family gets pretty wacky sometimes. Our idea of fun is having icing fights, going bowling and finding a new way to roll the ball each frame, or creating a nightlight with fireflies in a jar. Not many people are as zany as we are, but be creative in your fun.

Sometimes in marriage it feels like something is missing, like the lost final piece of a jigsaw puzzle. Often, that missing piece is simply having fun. Don't be too serious. Lighten up. Laugh. Be downright silly sometimes, because fun is an essential part of a healthy marriage.

THOUGHT FOR THE DAY

"A cheerful heart is good medicine, but a crushed spirit dries up the bones" (Proverbs 17:22).

TODAY'S ACTIVITY

Fun doesn't come naturally to everyone, and if you're among that group, share with your spouse any childhood experiences or teaching you had that might inhibit your ability to cut loose. Next, share with one another the top three fun experiences of your life. Finally, plan something fun for the near future, or just do something spontaneous.

A couple that plays together stays together. Find a day a week to do something fun together.
@RyanPMoore

NINE

KNOW ANY GIANTS?

Find some knowledgeable and trustworthy mentors.

Isaac Newton was one of the world's most brilliant scientists, and he contributed much to the world in the areas of mathematics, gravitation, optics, and other sciences. Yet he once wrote in a letter, "If I have seen further [than others], it is by standing upon the shoulders of Giants."

Even the best of us need guidance, advice, and other help. When it comes to having the best possible marriage, where do you look? You might start with a review of those who attended your wedding. Those who showed up clearly care for you, and young people tend to focus first on friends their own age. But resist the convenience of seeking advice from people at the same point in the journey. Newlyweds getting advice from other newlyweds is like two five-year-olds teaching each other to ride a bike—way too may spills and not nearly enough progress!

Some of the older guests at your wedding have much to offer (and perhaps many of those who couldn't make it). Some may have been modeling the ideal marriage for decades without your ever noticing it. It's time for you to start noticing!

Look for examples and advice from couples who:

Love you and have your best interests at heart;

Are ahead of you in the journey and have learned from their mistakes;

Are consistent in their treatment of others during good times and bad;

Have earned your admiration;

Have weathered life's storms and drawn closer together as a result;

Have had long-term success (twenty-five years or more).

Find trustworthy mentors. Listen to them. Learn from them. Then stand on their shoulders as you face the future together and become a couple that others will someday learn from.

THOUGHT FOR THE DAY

"The way of fools seems right to them, but the wise listen to advice" (Proverbs 12:15).

TODAY'S ACTIVITY

Think back to the people in your life who have set a consistently good example for you, especially in how to be a loving and caring spouse. Tell your spouse about each person and each lesson learned. Then write a short note to everyone you think of, thanking them for the groundwork they laid for your marriage (even if you recently wrote to thank them for a wedding gift). You have no idea what your note will mean to them.

If you want to succeed now and in the future, study the lives of those who have succeeded in their past and present.
@Aaron_Hlavin

TEN

YOU MAKE THE CALL

Call your own fouls.

Wouldn't it be great if you had a marriage referee? Whenever your spouse said something totally insensitive or did something wrong, a guy in a black-and-white striped shirt would blow a whistle, make a hand signal, and loudly announce the foul.

But since the job doesn't exist (yet), you need to resort to the playground rules of childhood where players call their own fouls. It's pretty clear when someone jumps offside in football or double dribbles in basketball. The foul is called, the player fesses up, and the game continues.

Consider some of the potential fouls you might call from the marriage rulebook:

False Start—"You promised three times to get that chore done, but I'm not seeing any progress."

Piling On—"I don't mind doing a favor or two for you, but remember how busy I am too before you ask so much of me."

Unnecessary Roughness—"Please lower the volume and calm down. We can work this out like adults."

Unsportsmanlike Conduct—"You totally ignored me after you saw your friends at the party."

Delay of Game—"We seem to be late for most of our commitments because you aren't ready on time."

Encroachment—"I love you to death, but sometimes I need a little 'me time.'"

Traveling—"You've been away from home an awful lot lately. I miss you."

After dealing with one or more of these issues and clearing the air, there's always one other call you can make, repeatedly, which you both should agree to: *holding*.

THOUGHT FOR THE DAY

"Search me, God, and know my heart; test me and know my anxious thoughts. See if there is any offensive way in me, and lead me in the way everlasting" (Psalm 139:23–24).

TODAY'S ACTIVITY

Spend some time in casual conversation, alerting your spouse to potential "fouls" you're likely to make under stress. Give the other person permission to call you on those things in the future if you don't do so yourself.

Playground rules rule. Respect your mate enough to hear them out, to keep the game moving forward and to keep it fun.
@andrewtempleton

ELEVEN

KEEPING UP BEATS CATCHING UP

Determine the habits you want to establish, and start now.

An experienced teacher once told me, "You can't let students do anything the first day of school that you don't want them to do the rest of the year."

The same general rule holds true for the first days of marriage. You need to start the habits you want to establish . . . now! Oh, I know. Money is always short. It's a hassle to get your schedules worked out. You have your whole life ahead of you to make up for lost time. But what young couples seldom realize is that time and money just keep getting tighter as you go along. As hard as it is to find a healthy balance for everything right now, it's never going to get easier.

Church involvement should be a given. Even though you're young and ambitious and others seem to be working around the clock, God has called us to a weekly period of rest for fellowship with Him and one another. Start now.

Giving is important. You may think that a fraction of your weekly income is such a paltry amount no one would ever notice. Yet Jesus noticed not only the widow's two small coins, but also her attitude (Luke 21:1–4). Start now.

Invest in others. As little as you may have, others have less. Find ways to help the disadvantaged, feed the hungry, or otherwise serve your community. Start now.

Meanwhile, *spend time with one another* to strengthen your marriage. Cindy and I enjoy walking together in the morning. We talk about the day before, the day ahead, and anything that comes to mind. Do what works for you, but start now.

THOUGHT FOR THE DAY

"Encourage one another daily, as long as it is called 'Today,' so that none of you may be hardened by sin's deceitfulness" (Hebrews 3:13).

TODAY'S ACTIVITY

Each spouse should determine two habits you would like to establish in your marriage—one rather easy to initiate and the other more challenging. Then discuss when and how you can incorporate those things into your regular schedule. (Do this again on occasion as you learn to manage your time.)

Though seemingly insignificant now, the shared rhythms of your daily life and marriage will set your course. Be intentional.
@NathanKollar

TWELVE

THERE'LL BE SOME CHANGES

You may as well enjoy change because you can't prevent it.

Even though it's early in your marriage, I suspect you've already established "your" seat at the kitchen table and "your" side of the bed. Those aren't likely to change. If you don't believe me, try swapping and see what happens.

Yet change will be essential for a growing marriage because the world is continually changing. The average American born in the nineties will hold eight different jobs in his or her lifetime and live in thirty different homes. We live in a world that just keeps spinning!

We are indeed creatures of habit. As difficult as it will be to change habits you've developed over your lifetime, growth in your marriage relationship will require regular change—new ways of doing things when the old ways don't work as well as you wish.

If your budget isn't working, you may need to change jobs or spending patterns. When jobs change or your work schedule shifts, you may need to change your prayer time and your date night. When your date night shifts, you can look for new and different ways to express appreciation and love for one another. And just when you get everything balanced and running smoothly, along come kids and everything is up for grabs again.

One change frequently leads to another, and that's not always a bad thing. It keeps you out of ruts and able to discern new opportunities you might otherwise have missed. Learning to live together and love each other is an ongoing process. If something isn't working, try something else. And as you do, don't forget to smile!

THOUGHT FOR THE DAY

"Because of the LORD's great love we are not consumed, for his compassions never fail. They are new every morning; great is your faithfulness" (Lamentations 3:22–23).

TODAY'S ACTIVITY

Prepare to practice change tomorrow. Whatever you usually do, plan something different. Be creative: eat outside; trade chores; watch a different TV show; etc.

Don't get stuck; deny the rut.
#practiceCHANGE
@Jennifer_McAfee

THIRTEEN

MONEY MATTERS

Commit to financial accountability.

You don't need to talk to a lot of young couples to discover how widespread is the problem of money management. Our culture promises easy credit, low monthly payments, buy now and pay later. Before you know it, you're neck deep in debt. You don't ever want to be in that position—and especially not early in a marriage.

So I urge you to establish a financial margin—a rainy-day fund available to you rather than ever-present debt. Think of driving on a highway. When you have both lanes to yourself and wide margins, you can enjoy the scenery. But if you're squeezed between a concrete divider and a semi-truck, you can't relax. Your car still takes the same amount of space, but the difference is that you have less margin for error, less room to act in case of an emergency. Financial margin takes off pressure, giving you room to maneuver a little without fearing an imminent wreck in the event of a minor mistake or unexpected expense.

Establishing sufficient financial margin is a marriage-preserving strategy. So save money! Here's how:

Give to God first. Next set aside your savings and investment. Then spend from what remains.

Resist the temptation to have everything right now. Never incur credit card debt.

Don't try to keep up with what other young couples have. When they have loads of debt, you'll more than catch up with paid-for stuff!

I've seen more marriages wreck because of money problems than anything else. Live below your means, and you'll always have margin. You're also far more likely to have marital harmony.

THOUGHT FOR THE DAY

"I have learned the secret of being content in any and every situation, whether well fed or hungry, whether living in plenty or in want. I can do all this through him who gives me strength" (Philippians 4:12b–13).

TODAY'S ACTIVITY

Debt frequently results from wanting things you don't have. So, today, spend a respectable amount of time listing the many things you *do* have that you truly care about. As you compile your list, discuss how the two of you can become content at this state of your marriage without over-spending in an attempt to acquire even more.

Have the "money talk." This is where you talk and decide as a couple how you will manage the money God's given you to steward.

@pastorjoecyr

FOURTEEN

TRADITION!

Establish family traditions.

In a classic scene from *Fiddler on the Roof,* Tevye speaks (and sings) of the significance of tradition in the history of his people. His was a Jewish upbringing, but tradition is important to the Christian faith as well. And traditions make marriages even more special.

One of the things I regret is that our family has established very few traditions. Ministries like mine are filled with unscheduled emergencies and very full weekends, which are my primary work times. It's challenging to make and keep traditions under such conditions, yet now that I am learning how special they can be, I wish I had tried harder.

Start your own traditions early as anchor points for your marriage, and later your family. You can start with something as small as eating chocolate chip pancakes for breakfast on Memorial Day, or making homemade pizza for Thanksgiving. You might now be having "macaroni Mondays" as an economic necessity, but that would be a good tradition to keep after you can afford much better fare. Your traditions don't have to be big, expensive, elaborate, or meaningful to others. They are *your* traditions. Start them now, and in thirty years your kids will look back on them as special times together.

THOUGHT FOR THE DAY

"Let us consider how we may spur one another on toward love and good deeds, not giving up meeting together, as some are in the habit of doing, but encouraging one another—and all the more as you see the Day approaching" (Hebrews 10:24–25).

TODAY'S ACTIVITY

Discuss with your spouse the traditions your family had when you were growing up and whether you want to continue any of those things as a couple. Also consider any of the things you two are already doing on a regular basis, even this early in your relationship. Do you want to commit to any of those (perhaps silly) activities as a family tradition?

Try to do things differently than you've ever seen them done before. Your marriage is more than the sum of your experiences.
@ryandarrow

FIFTEEN

GOING THE EXTRA (S)MILE

Transform "ordinary" into "fun."

"I'll have the usual."

"It's vacation time again. Want to go to the same cabin the same week?"

"Don't you think we're getting a little old for [fill in the blank]?"

I am aware that in the previous devotion I urged you to start family traditions, so you may think today's advice is contradictory. But there's a big difference between doing something on a regular basis because it's meaningful to you and getting into a rut. I believe the strongest marriages are those that are filled with rut-busting fun.

I could write an entire book on the crazy things our family has done to make life more interesting, but I will limit myself to one example: our annual Christmas card. It seems like everyone was sending the same picture at Christmas—the family in front of the fireplace with the dog. Not us. Every year, we dream up a wacky way to say "Merry Christmas." Previous Christmas photos have shown us:

Having an icing fight while making sugar cookies;

Underwater, on the moon, and at the pyramids (thanks to green screens and photo-shopping);

Dressed in Christmas sweaters while driving four-wheelers through a huge mud puddle;

Decorating each other with ornaments and lights;

Wearing superhero onesie pajamas;

And this year look for us in matching "sock monkey" outfits.

We always include a "regular" picture on the inside of the card, but first we have tremendous fun dreaming up something new and different.

Don't settle for the ordinary or mundane. Look for ways throughout your day to do something crazy, fun, and unexpected!

THOUGHT FOR THE DAY

"Be joyful in hope, patient in affliction, faithful in prayer" (Romans 12:12).

TODAY'S ACTIVITY

Review the previous week in search of missed opportunities to turn "ordinary" into "fun." People tend to do the normal, expected thing without much thought, when a conscious decision to do something out of the ordinary would have created a special moment. As you become more aware of missed opportunities, you'll identify similar situations in the future when you have another chance.

Your marriage should be creative and fun. Don't settle for ordinary. Do the unexpected. Surprise each other.
@randyjumper

SIXTEEN

LAUGH AT THAT PERSON IN THE MIRROR.

Don't take yourself too seriously.

I preached a great message one Sunday morning. It was a thought-provoking talk: creative, funny, and spiritual. When it was done, I was convinced it ranked as one of my top ten best.

That same afternoon I was walking through the student ministry lobby on the way to the sanctuary when one of the students stopped me. "Pastor Rod, I really noticed something while you were preaching this morning." I was so excited. I knew I had nailed the message, and he got it! I wondered what he had discovered that would change his life. I asked, "What did you learn?" He said: "Your sideburns are uneven."

I had become a little too full of myself, so I deserved to be deflated a bit. Before long, though, I realized how truly funny his comment was. If I hadn't been able to laugh at myself (eventually), that would have been a sad situation indeed. But God often uses the comically humbling incidents in life to remind us that we aren't nearly as essential as we believe we are.

Each day is filled with opportunities to laugh, and if you can't find anything better to chuckle about, laugh at your own miscues and embarrassing moments. And don't let yourself forget about them. Write them down, take a picture, or memorialize them in some other way. The lessons will be just as valid each time you review them . . . and just as funny.

THOUGHT FOR THE DAY

"When pride comes, then comes disgrace, but with humility comes wisdom" (Proverbs 11:2).

TODAY'S ACTIVITY

It's one thing to say you should be able to laugh at yourself, but often quite another to feel natural doing so. Rate yourself on a scale of 1 (least) to 10 (most) as to how comfortable you feel about laughing at yourself. What qualifications would you make? (Is it harder to do so at work than at home? Do certain family members frown on self-deprecation?)

Married life is awesome, and we should take it seriously because God does. But always enjoy what makes you laugh.
@MikeBurnette

SEVENTEEN

PICK YOUR BATTLES

Choose (and limit) your arguments.

Even though you're young-and-in-love newlyweds, you may have discovered by now that you'll still have occasional arguments and disagreements. Combining two lives, with your different family backgrounds and ways of doing things, can create tension. Although you can't avoid all conflicts, you *can* learn how to handle them.

My best advice is to determine in advance what you will argue about. Way too many marriage-altering and even marriage-ending disagreements start over things that simply don't matter. On matters of personal preference, be quick to give in to the other's wishes. Mutual submission helps prevent mutually assured destruction!

Cindy and I have very few arguments. I have opinions, but rarely voice them on things like the color of the wall, what kind of furniture we have, what to eat, etc. None of that should result in harsh words or hurt feelings. But as the leader and spiritual head of my family I will strongly assert my opinion if an issue:

Affects the long-term spiritual development of our family;

Violates our core values;

Negatively affects my ministry; or

Negatively affects our long-term financial future.

If an issue isn't in one of those four areas, I generally choose to submit to Cindy's wishes. Whenever I find myself arguing about things that don't really matter, I usually end up regretting it. But for the most part, we avoid arguments. Learn to choose your battles, and you can too.

THOUGHT FOR THE DAY

"Keep your servant also from willful sins; may they not rule over me. Then I will be blameless, innocent of great transgression" (Psalm 19:13).

TODAY'S ACTIVITY

Create a list together of what you think is worth arguing about, and revise it as needed. Eventually, you should agree that if an issue isn't on that list, you'll consider it irrelevant and not worth expending the energy to discuss. As a result, your marriage will be much happier—and easier!

"In essentials unity, in nonessentials liberty, and in all things charity" is also great marriage advice!
@RachelLBRoss

EIGHTEEN

REAL WEALTH

**Focus more on creating good memories
than acquiring possessions.**

At this early point in your marriage you are probably in a "settling in" phase. The wedding is past, the honeymoon but a fond memory. Now it's time to get back to work, which is a good and responsible thing to do. But while you're making a living, it's just as important to start making memories. Don't let your work responsibilities overshadow your relationship responsibilities.

After twenty-seven years of marriage, Cindy and I don't have any precious possessions, but we have lots of precious memories. I wouldn't have it any other way because while material things get lost, burn up, rot, mold, wither, fade, break, or expire, memories only deepen. In a short time, your memories of time together will be worth far more to you than anything you own.

Even challenging moments can yield priceless memories. Early in our marriage Cindy's car was wrecked *at the dealership*. Who else has their car totaled at the shop? The service manager was way more worried than we were. It would have been easy to become stressed, but instead we started laughing. More than twenty years later, we still laugh as we remember how Cindy made the dealer gather everything out of her car and put it in a bag so she wouldn't have the emotional trauma of seeing her wrecked Maxima. She literally wouldn't look at it!

Make your own memories. Write down the stories. You'll tell them and retell them. They become part of the history you'll pass down to the next generations— and a priceless inheritance.

THOUGHT FOR THE DAY

"Remember your Creator in the days of your youth, before the days of trouble come and the years approach when you will say, 'I find no pleasure in them'" (Ecclesiastes 12:1).

TODAY'S ACTIVITY

If you haven't done so already, begin a written record of the special moments you've already shared together. Right now you think you'll always remember, but years from now you'll be thankful you took time to record the dates and specifics to look back on.

Don't fill your life with things for future garage sales. Instead, fill your life with things money can't buy . . . memories.
@RyanPMoore

NINETEEN

"MY BAD!"

Admit and learn from mistakes.

I wish couples spent a fraction of the time preparing for marriage that they spend preparing for the wedding, but that's probably never going to happen. Still, it's important to develop a quick learning curve as you move along as a couple, and one of the first things to learn is how to get past mistakes.

You would like your spouse to go on believing that you're the world's first perfect husband/wife, but it's a given that you'll make mistakes—lots of them! With that in mind, here's my short list for "How to Manage Mistakes":

Admit it. **Sooner is better, and it's preferable to admit your mistake before getting caught and called on it.**

Own it. **Don't try to make excuses or you only encourage the other person to investigate.**

Seek forgiveness. **Apologize. Say, "I'm sorry." Those are powerful, argument-stopping words when said in the right spirit.**

Fix it. **Whatever it takes, make it right.**

Learn from it. **Ask yourself: Why did I do that? How can I avoid making that mistake again?**

Don't repeat it! **Repeating the same mistake is called a pattern. (I'll have more to say on this particular step in the next devotion.)**

It's naïve and foolish to think you'll avoid mistakes and subsequent conflicts. It's far better to anticipate mistakes and have a plan for how to deal with them. Next to perfection, honesty about one's shortcomings is perhaps the most attractive trait you can offer your spouse.

THOUGHT FOR THE DAY

"Praise the LORD, my soul, and forget not all his benefits—who forgives all your sins and heals all your diseases, who redeems your life from the pit and crowns you with love and compassion, who satisfies your desires with good things so that your youth is renewed like the eagle's" (Psalm 103:2–5).

TODAY'S ACTIVITY

Take turns finishing this statement: "I've really been hoping you wouldn't find out about . . ." Then use the steps from today's devotion to find resolution for the prior mistake you just revealed.

Your spouse knows you're not perfect and the sooner you realize it, too, the better.
@Aaron_Hlavin

TWENTY

A BREATH OF FRESH ERROR

Don't make the same mistakes; make new ones.

As hard as it may be to believe, I'm not a perfect husband. I've made a lot of mistakes. But I try to do as I urged you in the previous devotion, to learn from each mistake and avoid making the same mistake over and over. I thought I would share a personal example with you.

A few years ago, Cindy needed an operation to remove her gallbladder. She was clearly upset, so I asked, "What are you nervous about?" She said, "That I won't wake up." Being the sensitive, caring husband I am, I replied, "You'll wake up somewhere, either here or in heaven." (That was Mistake #1.)

Cindy said: "I would miss you and the boys." I said, in a far-too-sarcastic voice, "Really? You would say, 'Thanks, God. Great to be here, but I really miss Rod and the boys, so may I go back?'" (That was Mistake #2.)

Cindy was trying to be serious: "What would you do if something happened to me?" I said, "We would name the church nursery after you." (Strike #3; I was out.)

Cindy didn't laugh. I was repeatedly offering insensitive, smart-aleck comments when she clearly wanted and needed sympathy and support. Trust me, I learned from my mistake: pre-surgery is not the time for humor! If Cindy ever has surgery again, I'll be kind, gentle, understanding, and affirming.

Making the same mistakes over and over again constitutes a pattern, which should be avoided. But it's okay to make new ones because we keep learning from the mistakes we make. Be a couple that keeps your mistakes fresh and your forgiveness flowing.

THOUGHT FOR THE DAY

"If your brother or sister sins against you, rebuke them; and if they repent, forgive them. Even if they sin against you seven times in a day and seven times come back to you saying, 'I repent,' you must forgive them" (Luke 17:3–4).

TODAY'S ACTIVITY

Examine your own life (and your spouse's, if asked) for patterns of making the same mistakes. If you find a pattern, work on a team strategy for breaking it and preventing any further recurrence of the same mistake. If no patterns are evident, good for you! In that case, spend your time recalling and sharing your most recent "new" mistake(s)—and what you learned from each one.

Words give life and take life away. Sarcasm only takes away. Seek to build bridges in your words; not create pitfalls.
@andrewtempleton

TWENTY-ONE

FOREVER . . .
ONE MOMENT AT A TIME

Live in each moment, but keep looking ahead.

If you took traditional marriage vows, you and your spouse made a commitment to one another regardless of what might happen in the future: for better or worse . . . for richer or poorer . . . in sickness or in health. When most young people make that promise, they're usually counting on a lot more riches and health than poverty and sickness, but life holds no guarantees. I'm sure you've seen certain older couples who subsist on such meager incomes you wonder how they survive, and others where one spouse lovingly nurses the other through seemingly perpetual illness.

The couples who persevere through the difficulties of life are usually those who have a "forever" focus. They store memories of all the wonderful moments in their past and present, but they continue to look ahead as their love for one another fuels hope and optimism.

Other than a decision to follow Jesus, marriage is the only other forever-commitment you'll make, and thinking about forever will help you see life through a long lens. If you really believe "forever" starts on your wedding day, you're able to sidestep minor irritations and plow through major challenges of the moment.

To newlyweds, forever seems like a really long time. But Cindy and I aren't quite to the twenty-eight-years mark, and already forever seems but a blink. So make the most of each day. Live life to the fullest. Anytime things get scary, difficult, or uncomfortable, remember that you have forever to overcome the problem(s) together.

THOUGHT FOR THE DAY

"He has made everything beautiful in its time. He has also set eternity in the human heart; yet no one can fathom what God has done from beginning to end" (Ecclesiastes 3:11–12).

TODAY'S ACTIVITY

Discuss with your spouse all of your current challenging situations (financial, emotional, spiritual, vocational, etc.). Which are causing you the most concern at this point? How might it make a difference to view each of those troubling circumstances through a long lens . . . to put them in the context of forever?

In marriage, daily offer one another the wondrous gift of an everlasting, secure, & grace-infused covenant relationship.
@NathanKollar

TWENTY-TWO

PROPORTION AND DISTORTION

Check your motives to maintain a clear and
accurate perspective of your spouse.

I recently attended an event that had a printed program. The program was well-written, but there was one problem. All the photos were distorted because the aspect ratio of the pictures was off. Aspect ratio is the proportional relationship between an image's length and width. When the aspect ratio is not preserved, a good picture is stretched and twisted. So throughout this program were pictures of the "honored guests" that were to be acknowledged, but it was like seeing them in a funhouse mirror at a carnival.

If you don't preserve the "aspect ratio" of your marriage, something good can quickly be misperceived. Perception is easily twisted whenever you assume motives that aren't accurate.

Let's say your spouse does a major housecleaning while you're out because you have allergies and (s)he really wants to do something beneficial for you. But you learn that in the cleaning frenzy, (s)he took a favorite item of yours among the boxes (s)he carried to Goodwill. It was an item your mother gave you, so you start thinking, *I knew (s)he never cared for my mother*. Even if you don't mention the perceived offense, your marriage will suffer because you've assumed a wrong motive. The aspect ratio gets distorted, and you don't see your spouse clearly.

To keep the right "aspect ratio" and minimize criticism and hurt feelings, always assume that your spouse's motive is good and for your benefit. Give him/her credit for wanting you to be the very best you can be. Communicate clearly. And leave the funhouse mirrors at the carnival!

THOUGHT FOR THE DAY

"All a person's ways seem pure to them, but motives are weighed by the LORD. Commit to the LORD whatever you do, and he will establish your plans" (Proverbs 16:2–3).

TODAY'S ACTIVITY

Think back across your life to a time when you made a wrong assumption about someone and caused a relationship to suffer as a result. After you and your spouse share your stories with one another, prayerfully ask God to keep your thoughts pure as to each other's motives so that your relationship never undergoes unnecessary strain.

Perception is imagination playing tricks on you. Truth is reality. #communicate #clarity
@Jennifer_McAfee

TWENTY-THREE

"GOOD ENOUGH" USUALLY ISN'T

Don't settle for less than extraordinary.

A jewelry store in Central Arkansas runs a commercial with the tag line: "Life's too short for ordinary jewelry." The message subtly suggests that if you buy jewelry elsewhere, you're missing something really special. It's a good, memorable hook.

I think we need similar good reminders that, as followers of Christ, life's too short for "ordinary" in a lot of areas. A few pages back I encouraged you to transform "ordinary" into "fun" whenever you can. In many cases, though, it's less a matter of fun than of creating a truly extraordinary and ongoing experience.

I might start with the obvious: Life's too short for an ordinary marriage. Surely you've seen plenty of those—couples who seem to trudge on with no apparent signs of growth or enthusiasm. Determine to love each other more and better every day. Build an extraordinary life together!

Life's too short for ordinary expressions of love. Practice saying "I love you" in imaginative ways. Write it on the mirror in lipstick. Mow it into the yard. One time after a heavy rain while on a beach vacation, I stomped out "I Love You" in huge letters in the sand so Cindy could see it from our hotel window. Be creative!

Above all, life's too short to be an ordinary servant of God. We serve a living, all-powerful, loving and merciful God. How does that ever become *ordinary*? Take my word for it: When you're living for Him, life is plenty long for the ordinary events of daily life to transform into an extraordinary lifetime.

THOUGHT FOR THE DAY

"And whatever you do, whether in word or deed, do it all in the name of the Lord Jesus, giving thanks to God the Father through him" (Colossians 3:17).

TODAY'S ACTIVITY

Put your heads together and write your own list of "Life's too short for . . ." statements. Discuss any inclination you've noticed at this early stage in your marriage to settle for less than you should. How would you respond to someone who suggests, "Oh, you're doing good enough for now," or, "Hey, if it ain't broke, don't fix it?"

Wake up every day and make the decision to live it to the fullest; forgive past mistakes, and live today like it's your last.
@pastorjoecyr

TWENTY-FOUR

ENTITLEMENT VS. GRATITUDE

Rather than feeling entitled,
feel and express gratitude . . . often!

Sometimes a couple gets married, buys a home, settles into society, and starts feeling entitled. Some have grown up that way and may not know better. Others think the pretense of wealth and sophistication will eventually become the real thing. What such people usually don't realize is how hollow life can be under a façade of entitlement. Nothing ever seems to be enough. Actions are mechanical rather than genuine. Worst of all, when you see something as an entitlement, as something you *deserve*, you lose the art of gratitude.

It's much better to learn genuine appreciation. This starts with the realization of how blessed you are, that without the grace of God you would have nothing. And from that inner acknowledgement, gratitude spreads with outward expression. Saying "thank-you" every time someone does something for you is quickly becoming a lost art, but I hope your generation will reverse the trend.

In your marriage, gratitude keeps you from taking each other for granted. Learn to say thanks for little things as well as big things. The "I deserve" attitude is poison to a marriage. Fight it with all you've got!

An entitlement mentality takes the joy out of life. Gratitude is the antidote that spreads joy instead. As you and your new spouse get better at expressing thanks to one another, extend your gratitude to other family members, to coworkers, to salespeople, and to everyone else.

Say "thank-you" often. Document your thanks with texts, or better yet, written notes. Be extravagant in your words of thanks and stay away from the spoiled attitude of entitlement.

THOUGHT FOR THE DAY

"Let the message of Christ dwell among you richly as you teach and admonish one another with all wisdom through psalms, hymns, and songs from the Spirit, singing to God with gratitude in your hearts" (Colossians 3:16).

TODAY'S ACTIVITY

Make a list of at least ten things that you appreciate about your spouse that you've failed to express thanks for recently. Trade your lists, and then commit to keep the thank-yous coming during this next week.

Wanting your spouse, rather than needing them, is a powerful form of intimacy. Two "haves" don't make a whole.
@ryandarrow

TWENTY-FIVE

THE BALANCING ACT

Regularly turn your focus outward.

One of the hardest challenges for a family is finding the right balance between protecting yourselves and reaching out to others. You want to keep your family safe from the threats of this world, yet you also have an assignment from Jesus to influence those around you as salt and light.

One of the best ways to eventually keep your children safe is to start now, as a couple, developing an intentional outward focus. Otherwise your marriage will be subject to inertia that keeps you isolated. Resist that with all you've got! Try these ideas to get started:

Give Together. **In addition to your tithe, set aside a portion of your income for missions and the needs of others.**

Share Your Home. **Some of our most precious memories are almost two decades of "Family Nights" when we hosted good friends or others who needed to experience healthy family interaction.**

Serve Together. **Get out of the house altogether and find an opportunity to minister together.**

If you begin your outward focus now, and continue as kids are added to the family, they will automatically sense where the appropriate lines should be drawn between helping others and "stranger danger." When Jesus first sent disciples out with an outward focus, He told them, "I am sending you out like sheep among wolves. Therefore be as shrewd as snakes and as innocent as doves" (Matthew 10:16). Now there's a balancing act!

But Jesus also tells us, "Where your treasure is, there your heart will be also" (Matthew 6:21). Keep investing in others and watch your heart follow.

THOUGHT FOR THE DAY

"Do not store up for yourselves treasures on earth, where moths and vermin destroy, and where thieves break in and steal. But store up for yourselves treasures in heaven, where moths and vermin do not destroy, and where thieves do not break in and steal. For where your treasure is, there your heart will be also" (Matthew 6:19–21).

TODAY'S ACTIVITY

Start discussing the best ways you might work together to turn your focus outward. Start with local needs you already know about, but later follow up with your church leaders to see what other opportunities might be open to you.

Your home is more than a sanctuary; it's where your family learns compassion and generosity. Reach out; it's worth the risk.
@randyjumper

TWENTY-SIX

VIVE LA DIFFÉRENCE

Appreciate your spouse's unique, God-designed differences.

I am an ESPN-watching, almost-always-active, introverted guy who hates parties. I married a Lifetime channel-watching, relaxed, outgoing woman who loves to go out to any kind of get-together. And believe it or not, we're a fairly typical pair.

As I counsel with couples, one question I ask is: "What caused you to fall in love with him/her in the first place? What was the attraction?" Their answers reflect the truth that opposites do indeed attract. Savers marry spenders. Rowdy personalities are attracted to quiet ones. Planners are drawn to a spontaneous mate.

For example, one of the things that drew me to Cindy was her fun-loving, extroverted, talk-to-anyone personality. But now when she strikes up a long conversation with the person behind us in line at the register, I get frustrated and impatient. Still, I don't try to change Cindy, and she doesn't try to change me. We love each other in spite of our differences. In fact, we probably love each other more *because of* our differences!

God may have put you with a complete opposite. If so, that's part of His design. He created you both to be the way you are, so celebrate your different strengths even as you realize those things may also create tension in your marriage at times. Allow the reasons you fell in love to be the reasons you stay in love!

I try to learn from Cindy's strengths. I'll probably never be as outgoing as she is, although I'm better than I was. But I still can't watch those silly, sappy movies on Lifetime!

THOUGHT FOR THE DAY

"There are different kinds of gifts, but the same Spirit distributes them. There are different kinds of service, but the same Lord. There are different kinds of working, but in all of them and in everyone it is the same God at work" (1 Corinthians 12:4–6)

TODAY'S ACTIVITY

It's about time for an update of the activity you did for Devotion #3. So once again, each of you make a list of the things you like best about your spouse. (By now you should have discovered some new insights to include.) Share your lists with one another and then determine a fun way to celebrate as your marriage begins to flourish.

Be thankful that your spouse is not like you. One of the coolest things in marriage is to complement each other.
@MikeBurnette

TWENTY-SEVEN

LOSE THE SCOREBOARD

If you keep score, someone loses.

I love all kinds of sports. In most cases the scoreboard is an essential part of the game. Much of the coach's strategy is often determined by both the current score and how much time is left on the board. People watch games because they want to see who wins, and the scoreboard reveals a winner and a loser. Not many people would stay interested in a game where no one kept score.

Having said that, I also enjoy watching very young and totally inexperienced youngsters learn a sport. Soccer games are particularly enjoyable. No need for a scoreboard there, because no one bothers to keep score. Some games might be 0 to 0 the whole time, and others would be 67 to 59. Who cares? The kids are busy running and having a great time, and parents are busy shouting instructions to their children to do even the most basic things.

Your marriage should be much more like a kiddie soccer game than a professional sports contest. Far too many young husbands and wives start "keeping score":

"I gave you a great gift, and you got me that?"

"I mowed the lawn and fixed the car. What did you do?"

"We've visited your parents sixteen times this year and mine only fourteen."

If you keep score, marriage becomes a competition, and every competition has a winner and a loser. Why would you want to make the most important person in your life feel like a loser? If and when you do, trust me, you don't win!

Toss out the marriage scoreboard. Life is much more enjoyable if you just play for fun.

THOUGHT FOR THE DAY

"[Love] does not dishonor others, it is not self-seeking, it is not easily angered, it keeps no record of wrongs" (1 Corinthians 13:5).

TODAY'S ACTIVITY

Create a tongue-in-cheek "sportscast" that humorously reflects any of the ways you think keeping score might be creeping into your marital harmony. Read your sportscasts to one another, quickly forgive one another for any tendencies to keep score so far, and then commit only to play for fun from this point onward. If one of you reverts to keeping score in the future, it's time to call your own fouls. (See Devotion #10.)

Your heart cannot be simultaneously filled with someone's record of wrongs and record of greats. You choose.
@RachelLBRoss

TWENTY-EIGHT

WHEN THE "RIGHT WAY" IS WRONG

The "right way" to run a marriage is whatever works for you.

I have horrible allergies, which makes mowing the lawn an invitation to a day of absolute misery. I'm thankful we are finally able to afford someone to take care of our lawn, but for many years that luxury wasn't in our budget. Since mowing was "the man's job," I would wear a mask . . . and still get sick.

When Cindy saw how terribly sick I got after mowing, she decided it was time for a change. She asked (demanded, actually) to be the one who mowed the lawn, and I didn't fight too hard to disagree. Still, our mutual agreement bothered me. I always worried what other people would think if they drove by our house and saw my wife pushing a mower. Would they think I was lazy or a bad husband? Would they wonder about our marriage?

You'll discover no shortage of people who are quick to tell you the "right way" to run your marriage: the "right" division of household jobs; the "right" amount of time to spend together; or the "right" way to act. Instead of obsessing with what will look right to others, just decide what works best for the two of you. Every marriage is unique. What's right for your marriage will be entirely different from someone else's "right way."

I should mention . . . Cindy also has horrible allergies. She struggled every time she mowed the lawn. However, she knew I had to speak numerous times every week. She chose to get sick, so that I wouldn't. Now that's the right way to show love for a spouse!

THOUGHT FOR THE DAY

"For the LORD gives wisdom; . . . he guards the course of the just and protects the way of his faithful ones. Then you will understand what is right and just and fair—every good path" (Proverbs 2:6, 8–9).

TODAY'S ACTIVITY

Think long and hard about the routines you are establishing for your marriage. Do any of them need adjusting, even if a change might not seem "right" at first? In order to make your marriage as strong and enduring as possible, you both need to be honest with each other regarding your division of labor. In fact, you might even do some intentional "role reversal" on occasion, where husband and wife trade traditional chores. Try it and see what happens!

A healthy marriage is a lot like a road trip.
There are many routes to get there, but
each relationship has its unique road map.
@RyanPMoore

TWENTY-NINE

TEND TO YOUR CROPS

Strategically plan what you will plant.

My friend Robby is a farmer, and last year I asked him what he was planting. Robby knew exactly where he was planting corn, where he was plating rice, and where he was planting beans. He had a plan for when to plant, what to plant, and when to harvest.

Imagine the lunacy of going to the co-op for seeds and saying, "Surprise me. Just give me a variety and I'll toss them in the dirt. Nothing more fun than a surprise harvest." Only a foolish farmer would plant without a plan. Yet some people enter marriage without any kind of plan.

Planting is not accidental for either farming or family; it's intentional. If you don't have a plan for what you're going to plant in your marriage—the values, beliefs, traditions, and practices you hope to harvest someday—your spouse and later your children are in for a surprise harvest . . . but they won't like the surprise. If you don't have a planting plan, you are probably planting some wrong things.

A healthy marriage and a strong family will not grow by accident. They grow because you work together to determine the results you want, create a strategic plan, and then start planting the right seeds. Much work is still necessary during the stages of growth and cultivation, but at least you know you can expect your efforts to be fruitful. So first choose the harvest you hope to have, and then determine the seed.

THOUGHT FOR THE DAY

"Do not be deceived: God cannot be mocked. A man reaps what he sows"
(Galatians 6:7).

TODAY'S ACTIVITY

Sit down with your spouse and discuss the harvest you desire for your current marriage, and later for your family. Ask yourselves:

What do we want other people to see when they observe our marriage now?

What values do we want to be strong in our marriage by our twenty-fifth anniversary?

What core values do we want our children to develop and ultimately pass on to their children?

What specific "seeds" should we plant right now and how, precisely, do we do that?

Knowing what you want your marriage
to look like tomorrow, determines your
actions today.
@Aaron_Hlavin

THIRTY

SOS

Ask for help when you need it.

People thought the RMS *Titanic* was an unsinkable ship, yet when it struck the iceberg in the North Atlantic Ocean, it was just as dependent on a distress call as if it had been a schooner toppled by strong winds and high waves.

No marriage is immune from occasional stormy waters and uncontrollable gusts. All marriages face times when no amount of hard work and good intentions seem to be enough. Many times the difference in whether or not the marriage weathers a storm is the willingness of the couple to ask for help.

Why do so many people wait until a crisis to ask for help? *Pride.* They don't want anyone to know they're struggling with problems or searching for answers. But it's foolish to wait until water is pouring over the railings to start looking for a bucket. Ask for help whenever you want it and as often as you need it.

At every stage of marriage you'll face challenges that are new to you. To start with, I believe it's ministerial malpractice to perform a wedding without premarital counseling. If you haven't had at least five sessions to learn what to expect, start there. Later on, why act like you know how to raise an infant when you've never had one? Ask for help! Why would you pretend you understand adolescents? Ask for help! You'll regularly need advice from people who have been there already and know more than you.

No matter how hard you try, you won't be able to dodge all the icebergs out there. Have the flares ready to signal for help . . . and don't be afraid to use them!

THOUGHT FOR THE DAY

"Plans fail for lack of counsel, but with many advisers they succeed" (Proverbs 15:22).

TODAY'S ACTIVITY

Brainstorm together the type of help you might need at this stage in your marriage: spiritual counseling, schooling, scheduling, job advancement, home repair, etc. For every category that comes to mind, think of a couple of people who might be helpful. Look up their phone numbers and/or email addresses today and add them to your phone contacts or daily planners. Then you'll be ready for almost anything.

Utilize the experience of those near you. Don't travel the new road alone; take guides to show you the path and way forward.
@andrewtempleton

THIRTY-ONE

THE WORD AFTER "LOVE"

Honor your vow to honor one another.

"I take thee to be my wedded wife/husband, to have and to hold from this day forward, for better for worse, for richer for poorer, in sickness and in health, to love, honor, and cherish till death us do part, according to God's holy ordinance."

These wedding vows, still frequently used, actually date back to the *Book of Common Prayer* published in 1549. For hundreds of years, brides and grooms have made this promise to one another.

Today, when we talk about marriage, we say a lot about love but tend to overlook the word that comes next in the vow, *honor*. Sadly, honor is becoming a forgotten value in our society and our marriages. Honor is easy to detect but much harder to describe. You can feel honor. Others can sense it.

Honor is intentional. To honor your spouse is to determine:

You matter (which is something we all like to feel)!

I love you for who you are, not for what you do.

Your needs are more important than my desires.

I choose to put you first.

Honor requires more than words; it selflessly serves through frequent actions. One spouse committed to honor the other can change the environment of a home. But both persons committed to honor the other create a beautiful, lasting marriage. Choose to honor one another, "till death" you do part.

THOUGHT FOR THE DAY

"Be devoted to one another in love. Honor one another above yourselves" (Romans 12:10).

TODAY'S ACTIVITY

Finish this sentence and then read it to your spouse as a commitment: "From this point onward I choose to honor you, and by that I mean specifically that I will . . ."

Through developing a culture of honor in your marriage, you create an environment that sets one another up to fly.
@NathanKollar

THIRTY-TWO

YOU THINK *YOU'VE* GOT PROBLEMS? GOOD!

Let troubles bring you closer together.

I know a couple whose marriage has been challenged for over two decades with criticism, attacks, financial insufficiency, overwhelming medical expenses, uncertainty, fear, discouragement, betrayal, and many other challenges. That couple is Cindy and me. We recently celebrated our twenty-seventh anniversary, and we've never been happier. (I'm not sure what you're supposed to give at twenty-seven years . . . copper?)

I could tell lots of personal stories, but what they all teach is that the challenges of life seem to fade in light of the accumulated joy of a strong marriage. Looking back, the many difficult moments that seemed insurmountable, weren't.

You'll have some hard times. There will be struggles. But during the times of trouble you learn the power of commitment to each other and to God. Your relationship is strengthened by struggle as gold is purified by fire. So when trouble comes, remember:

No one is promised a trouble-free life, so no pity parties allowed!

You signed up for this. "For better or worse" is not a continual smooth ride.

This season won't last forever. You'll get through it.

People are watching to see how you respond to difficulty. This is a chance to prove your faith.

One day you'll look back and realize you are stronger because of your difficulties.

The good times far outnumber the bad times, so focus on the positive and celebrate blessings.

Endure each difficulty, grow stronger, and look with anticipation toward a wonderful copper anniversary someday!

THOUGHT FOR THE DAY

"In this world you will have trouble. But take heart! I have overcome the world" (John 16:33).

TODAY'S ACTIVITY

Memorize John 16:33. As troubles arise within and without your marriage in the next few days and weeks, remember to recite the verse as though Jesus is speaking directly to you. Soon you'll develop a new perspective on your troubles.

Marriage is worth the trouble. Struggle, tragedy, and heartache create compelling legacy. #toughLOVE #John16v33
@Jennifer_McAfee

THIRTY-THREE

ACCENTUATE THE POSITIVE

Focus on what you *will* be not on what you *won't* be.

When you're driving and you look at something on the right side of the road, do you know what your natural tendency is? You begin to pull the car toward the right. That same principle applies to much of life: You move toward what you focus on.

You may have the best of intentions as you begin to dwell on negative traits you want to avoid in your marriage, but thinking of those things actually works against you. A perpetual focus on the negative steers you in that direction, so it's far better to focus on positive goals. Let me give you a few examples:

Nice sentiment: "I'll never get a divorce."

Better focus: "I'll do whatever it takes to make my marriage strong. I'll attend classes, retreats, and seminars to keep our relationship growing."

Nice sentiment: "I won't be harsh like my father."

Better focus: "I'll be gentle and affirming with my spouse. I'll be understanding and loving in moments of failure and will celebrate moments of success."

Nice sentiment: "I won't be cold and distant like my parents."

Better focus: "I'll say 'I love you' to every member of my family every day. I'll hug them often and express verbally how much they mean to me."

Do you see the subtle difference? "I'll never get a divorce" or "I won't be harsh and demanding" are wonderful goals. The problem is, they include absolutely no action-steps to promote follow-through. Keep your eyes on positive goals and your marriage will never steer off course.

THOUGHT FOR THE DAY

"Let us throw off everything that hinders and the sin that so easily entangles. And let us run with perseverance the race marked out for us, fixing our eyes on Jesus, the pioneer and perfecter of faith" (Hebrews 12:1–2).

TODAY'S ACTIVITY

Sit down together and try to identify any "nice sentiments" you have about your marriage that may actually have a negative focus. Work together to revise your perspective so you have a better focus with clear action steps to keep you moving forward.

Use life-giving, positive, action words every day that will speak LIFE to what you will do to build up each other.
@pastorjoecyr

THIRTY-FOUR

PASS IT ON

When you find it hard to forgive,
recall how much you have been forgiven.

As you stand at the altar and take your vows, you like to think your forthcoming marriage will be trouble free. You know better, but still, you like to hope.

It's inevitable that over the course of marriage, and eventually parenting, you'll say and do things you shouldn't. You hurt others when you don't intend to, and when you *do*, your next step is crucial.

Some homes are ruled by *failure*. Spouses and/or parents become distant if another doesn't perform or respond as expected. In time, the lack of affirmation creates a mindset of failure. It's a terrible way to live.

No better are the homes ruled by *fear*. One spouse or parent can become domineering for any number of reasons—none of them valid. Sadly, others in the household learn to say what the person wants to hear, and when they fail to do so they are quick to cower or retreat.

The remedy for both problems is *forgiveness*. Everyone in the household needs to learn to forgive quickly and repeatedly. Each of us should be humbled if we put any thought into the forgiveness we receive continually from God. Nehemiah understood: *But you are a forgiving God, gracious and compassionate, slow to anger and abounding in love* (Nehemiah 9:17). What a beautiful description of a forgiving God—and it's the description we should all strive for as a spouse: forgiving, gracious, compassionate, slow to become angry and full of love.

Let those be your goals as you begin your marriage. Think often about God's incredible forgiveness, and then try to pass it along to others, beginning with those in your household.

THOUGHT FOR THE DAY

"Do not judge, and you will not be judged. Do not condemn, and you will not be condemned. Forgive, and you will be forgiven" (Luke 6:37).

TODAY'S ACTIVITY

Read and discuss Jesus' parable of the unmerciful servant in Matthew 18:21–35. Jesus used some extreme contrasts in this parable, but made a valid point. In what ways have you seen behavior not unlike the servant's in your own school, neighborhood, workplace, or (dare I even suggest it) church?

A marriage built on grace is a marriage full of new beginnings. Let your forgiveness be greater than your hurts.
@ryandarrow

THIRTY-FIVE

HOME IS WHERE THE AFFIRMATION IS

If you want to motivate someone, use affirmation rather than criticism.

I consider myself a fairly secure leader, but let me tell you a secret. I get about 850 emails each week. When I open my inbox, I first scan down the names of the senders looking for someone I know to be an encourager, and I open that email first because I like to feel good and I still need to be affirmed. I save every encouraging email, note, card, and letter. When I'm feeling a little down, or when people say cruel things, I reach into the file and randomly pull out something good to read. It changes my outlook.

Affirmation is a tremendous force. Everyone loves to be told they have done well, to be reminded that they matter. Telling your spouse everything that's wrong about him or her will never make your relationship better. Instead, become an intentional, outrageous affirmer.

Here is a powerful truth: You return to the places that make you feel affirmed. If you're treated nicely at a restaurant, you go back. If someone always has a kind word for you at church, you seek that person out every week.

The first crack in the foundation of most marriages that fail is a lack of affirmation. "My husband doesn't make me feel loved anymore." "My wife is never happy with me." Keep your foundation sure and strong by making it your goal to be the primary affirmer for your spouse. Make each other feel loved and affirmed in your home, and it will always be your favorite place.

THOUGHT FOR THE DAY

"May the God who gives endurance and encouragement give you the same attitude of mind toward each other that Christ Jesus had, so that with one mind and voice you may glorify the God and Father of our Lord Jesus Christ. Accept one another, then, just as Christ accepted you, in order to bring praise to God" (Romans 15:5–7).

TODAY'S ACTIVITY

Sometimes we need affirmation but don't know how to ask for it. Try to establish an "affirmation corner" or "affirmation seat" in a seldom-used portion of your home. From now on, whenever one spouse goes to the designated spot, it's a signal that he or she needs a little special attention from the other spouse. (And if you want to know more about how to create affirmation, move on to the next devotion.)

Be your spouse's greatest cheerleader! Create moments to tell your spouse how amazing he or she is.
@randyjumper

THIRTY-SIX

MAKE AN A IN AFFIRMATION

Celebration creates affirmation.

As a child, did you ever come home with a report card with 3 A's, 2 B's and a C? If so, how did your parents react? Unfortunately, many parents lead with a lecture on the need to bring up the C instead of celebrating the more numerous A's.

That's a natural tendency for people who spend a lot of time together. We dwell on one area that needs improvement instead of celebrating the many other areas of strength, growth, and progress. Over time we develop a horrible habit of spending a lot of time correcting and not a lot of time affirming, and we justify it in a lot of ways:

"I just want what's best for him."

"I don't want her to make the same mistakes I made."

"I'm saying things they need to hear."

These are often valid reasons, but people quickly tire of hearing correction. Why not try a different approach? Instead of blasting on the negative, celebrate the positive. Every day, look for something positive to celebrate in your spouse and watch your relationship grow happier and healthier! Affirmation is a powerful motivator for your marriage and family.

The world is full of people who will correct and criticize. You don't want to be just one more critic at home, do you? So cheer up . . . and start celebrating. Soon your spouse will rate you an A+!

THOUGHT FOR THE DAY

"Anxiety weighs down the heart, but a kind word cheers it up" (Proverbs 12:25).

TODAY'S ACTIVITY

Complete the following sentences for your spouse:

"I have missed affirming you lately, specifically in regard to these things you have done or achieved: _____

_____. And I plan to make it up to you by

_____."

Sticks & Stones break bones, & the words
we use CAN CRUSH each other. Your
spouse needs your words of grace.
@MikeBurnette

THIRTY-SEVEN

PAY BACK (IN A GOOD WAY)

Give whatever you hope to receive.

Suppose you've gotten lost in the desert on the hottest day of the year. You're beginning to get a little disoriented when you stumble upon an old farmhouse. No one is home, and the house has no utilities—no water. But out back is a rusty water pump beside which is half a jar of murky, insect-laden water. You're desperate. Do you drink it?

You might want to chug it right away . . . but that would be a mistake. Old pumps needed to be "primed." If you work the handle up and down as you pour that grotesque-looking liquid down the pump, a torrent of clean, fresh water will come gushing out the spout. When you finish drinking your fill, you leave the jar filled for the next lost soul who comes along.

It's much the same way with other essentials of life: give what little you have of something, and you're likely to receive much more in return. But you need to initiate the exchange:

If you want love, give love. You initiate it.

If you want affirmation, give affirmation. You go first.

If you want gratitude, give gratitude. You start.

If you want honor, give honor.

If you want kindness, give kindness.

And so on, and so on, and so on.

You get what you give, whether water at the pump or love in your marriage. The next time you want something, try giving it first. You'll discover that what you give comes back to you many times over. Just be sure to leave a little something for the next person who needs it.

THOUGHT FOR THE DAY

"One person gives freely, yet gains even more; another withholds unduly, but comes to poverty" (Proverbs 11:24).

TODAY'S ACTIVITY

Start simple. Take a walk with your spouse today where you are likely to come into contact with other people (your neighborhood, a mall, etc.). Whenever you see someone, smile and/or wave or speak to the person. Keep a tally to see how many of those people reply in kind. In coming days, move on to other qualities you would like to experience, and find a way to initiate those things with other people. I hope you're pleasantly surprised with the results.

"Freely we have received, freely give." God started the ball rolling, now we get to join in the fun!
@RachelLBRoss

THIRTY-EIGHT

THE COMPANY YOU KEEP

It's still essential to choose your friends carefully.

When you were kids, your parents probably told you "Choose your friends carefully." Wrong friends lead to wrong choices, wrong directions, and wrong results. Life can be dangerous for kids and adolescents if they're exposed to drinking, smoking, drug use, and all kinds of other dangerous behavior.

Now that you're married adults, I hope you still hear the voice of your parents with the same message. Choosing the people with whom you will have deep friendship is still just as important. Life can be dangerous for newlyweds if they're exposed to bitter divorcees, macho husbands, cynical wives, argumentative couples, or any number of other harmful influences.

Avoid people who are dissatisfied with their marriages. They'll speak dissatisfaction into yours. They project their unhappiness on you because your happiness reminds them of their misery. Listening to their negative, unhappy voices can create a subtle, creeping unhappiness with your own marriage.

It doesn't take a trained counselor to notice that people who are unhappy with their spouses tend to get together and talk about all their spouses' faults and failures. Don't fall into that discouraging trap!

When it comes to your closest, deepest friendships, carefully select couples who are positive about their own marriages and encouraging about yours. Being around happy people will help you stay happy! (And your parents will be so proud to know they taught you something valuable.)

THOUGHT FOR THE DAY

"The righteous choose their friends carefully, but the way of the wicked leads them astray" (Proverbs 12:26).

TODAY'S ACTIVITY

Working together, conduct a "friends inventory." List everyone you currently spend time with and evaluate each relationship. Which ones are the most positive . . . the ones you continue to talk about long after you've gone your separate ways? What specific lessons have those couples taught you about marriage? Which relationships, if any, might be potentially harmful to your marriage?

Are your closest friends adding value to your marriage? If not, they shouldn't be your closest friends.
@RyanPMoore

THIRTY-NINE

THE POWER OF WEAKNESS

Acknowledge your total dependence on God.

Lots of couples want to build healthy relationships, but where they look for advice makes all the difference in the world. Some depend on their existing levels of knowledge and/or experience, which is generally quite limited. Others follow faithfully the numerous TV gurus or peruse their local Barnes and Noble for the latest books on the topic.

Building a good marriage takes more than that. Much more. Don't be foolish. Now is not the time for pride. Admit your need for God. He has brought you together as a couple, and now you need to acknowledge your total *dependence* on Him to provide what you need throughout the good and the challenging times of your marriage.

It's a paradox. When you pretend to be strong, that's when you are most weak. But when you admit your human faults and weaknesses, and totally depend on God, that's when you are strong—not in your own power, but in His.

Don't be shocked when I tell you this, but your spouse already knows you aren't perfect. Your spouse knows you well enough by now to know when you're faking strength. But when your spouse sees you freely admit your need for God and His help, that's an action to be admired. That's not weakness. That's strength!

Don't be independent. Be God-dependent!

THOUGHT FOR THE DAY

"[The Lord] said to me, 'My grace is sufficient for you, for my power is made perfect in weakness.' Therefore I will boast all the more gladly about my weaknesses, so that Christ's power may rest on me. . . . For when I am weak, then I am strong" (2 Corinthians 12:9–10).

TODAY'S ACTIVITY

Admit your need for God both individually and together. Pray as a couple, using the following prayer to start and then adding what's on your heart. "God, we have a lot of faults and weaknesses. We make so many mistakes. There's a lot we don't know. But we do know this: we want to be together forever, faithfully following You. We need Your wisdom, Your help, and Your strength. We're completely and total dependent upon You."

Strength in marriage is overcoming your shortcomings together in humility.
@Aaron_Hlavin

FORTY

TIME . . . MORE OR LESS

Plan for time together.

The old song was true: "You can't hurry love." Relationships are developed in the context of shared time, and our most important relationships require the most time and attention.

I suspect you've been thinking, *Now that we're married, we'll get lots more time together*, but that's a mistake. The simple fact is that life gets busy. We're always busy, often too busy. It seems there are never enough hours in the day, or days in the week. If you don't plan time alone with the people you care about, it won't happen. (Society has gotten pretty good at pushing this point at parents who need to spend more time with children, but it should start with shared time between spouses.)

People have different approaches to this. Some couples have a date night every week. I like the concept, yet that's not possible for Cindy and me. So figure it out, do what works for you, plan it into your schedules, and then put it on your calendars.

You don't have to go into the evening with big plans and objectives. It doesn't have to be a production. Relax. Most of the time, do something you both enjoy (out for dinner, a movie, bowling, or whatever). But occasionally do something exclusively for the other spouse. (Guys, that may mean dressing up for theater or ballet. Ladies, that's probably going to include sports of some sort.)

It's a basic principle: what you work on grows; what you neglect dies. So don't neglect your marriage. When you get the hang of spending time together, neither of you will want to hurry your love.

THOUGHT FOR THE DAY

"A generous person will prosper; whoever refreshes others will be refreshed" (Proverbs 11:25).

TODAY'S ACTIVITY

You've been married a few months now. Discuss together: Do you see any trends in how much time you're spending together as a couple? Are you satisfied with your regular times together these days? If not, what can you do—right now—to remedy the problem? If so, what things can you do to ensure you'll continue to be content?

Lose the bedroom TV and talk instead. Quality time only comes through quantity. Create opportunities for deep communication.
@andrewtempleton

FORTY-ONE

FIX IT FAST

Resolve conflicts quickly.

Many businesses have learned a valuable (and profitable) lesson: If you want to stand out from the crowd, learn to respond quickly to a customer's wants, needs, and complaints. Overnight shipping. Car repair while you wait. Twenty-four-hour customer-service phone lines. The variations are endless. I wish more married couples would adopt the same principle: When problems arise, deal with them quickly.

When you save up, you blow up. Have you ever known someone like that? You two are talking and you think things are fine, then all of a sudden . . . *Whammo!* The person starts spewing everything that has ticked them off for the last six months. And if that person happens to be your spouse, it's a recipe for disaster (and some really long arguments).

It's inevitable that you'll have conflicts and disagreements, especially in marriage when you're so close and spend so much time around each other. Things will frustrate and irritate you (*and* your spouse). You should be honest about the way you feel, but you need to deal with conflicts as they arise. My friend, Alton Garrison, says it this way: "Don't gunnysack. Don't hold onto things and save them for later."

Stay current. Handle the little problems when they're still little, and they won't create major problems. But if you let them all lump together, you'll find yourself with a big mess.

Forgiveness: immediate delivery. That's something you can get used to.

THOUGHT FOR THE DAY

"Do not let the sun go down while you are still angry, and do not give the devil a foothold" (Ephesians 4:26–27).

TODAY'S ACTIVITY

Talk together and agree how you will attempt to resolve any future disagreements quickly. For example, some couples establish a bedtime deadline. If they have an argument, they come to terms (or at least call a truce) before going to bed. When they awaken, it's a new day and they can offer one another a fresh start. Whatever you decide to do, remember it the next time you disagree and put your plan into action.

Address conflicts in marriage quickly or else your roots will sink deep into the soil of contempt rather than love.
@NathanKollar

FORTY-TWO

THE BEST DEFENSE FOR A HARSH OFFENSE

Thicken your skin.

I remember one time when I offended someone terribly. What was my unforgivable, egregious offense? I didn't recognize his voice on the phone. When he asked, "Do you know who this is?" I didn't have a clue. He was actually hurt and offended.

You wouldn't believe the stories I could tell about the things that offend some people—the smallest, slightest, most insignificant things. And in almost every instance, as it was with my unidentified phone caller, the person *chose* to be offended.

I've discovered that the lower someone's maturity level, the more likely the person is to be offended. Because I'm committed to ongoing growth and maturity, you can't offend me. Instead, here is what happens. You say something hurtful to me, maybe something you shouldn't. After you do, I get to make a decision: I can decide to be offended, or I can choose to overlook it in love.

This one principle could change your marriage: Whenever you feel offended, you have a choice. Marital harmony is sometimes as simple as deciding not to be offended. What *isn't* as simple is that both of you need to make that choice *regularly*. In a mature marriage, both parties choose to overlook words or actions that could cause an offense.

In your workplace, neighborhood, school, and everywhere else you go, choose not to be offended. Quit being a baby. Grow up. And when you get home, that goes double. Cut your spouse some slack. Always give that person—the one you love the most—the benefit of the doubt.

THOUGHT FOR THE DAY

"A person's wisdom yields patience; it is to one's glory to overlook an offense" (Proverbs 19:11).

TODAY'S ACTIVITY

Grab a pen and paper and write down all the insensitive comments you can recall that have been directed at you recently, regardless how well you know the source. Review your list with your spouse, and be honest about how you felt in each instance. (It's natural to be hurt by rude and thoughtless people.) Ask your spouse to help you choose to forgive and forget each comment. And if you've been a source of offense to one another, be especially willing to forgive. Depending on how strongly you've been offended, however, some comments may require more prayer time than others before you can put the matter behind you.

Suck it up. Choosing offense is
self-preservation at the expense of
partnership. Build oneness, not selfishness.
#uGET2choose
@Jennifer_McAfee

FORTY-THREE

MORE EFFECTIVE PRAY-ERS

Grow closer by praying together.

You're almost at the halfway point in this book. So far I hope you've read (and perhaps learned) much about how to make your marriage stronger both physically and emotionally. But it's just as essential—indeed, even more so—to solidify the spiritual aspects of your marriage. If you want God to be involved in your relationship and development, you need to talk to Him.

Do you want intimacy in your marriage? Pray together! Nothing is more intimate than connecting together with your heavenly Father, who created your inmost beings (Psalm 139:13). Make prayer a regular, natural part of your life and relationship when one of you is sick, facing a big decision, stressed, blessed . . . all the time!

Imagine an equilateral triangle resting on one side with the point straight up. Think of God at that point and you and your spouse at the other two corners. Too often, couples struggle to get closer to one another with little regard for God. But if both of you make an effort to move closer to God, what happens? You can't help but get closer and closer to one another as well.

Prayer doesn't have to be a lengthy spiritual production. As you encounter daily challenges, pause and pray together a few simple sentences to ask for help and direction. When you have victories to celebrate, stop and pray to give thanks. Let talking to God *together* become a regular part of your life. The great thing is, He listens and answers!

THOUGHT FOR THE DAY

"Pray continually" (1 Thessalonians 5:17).

TODAY'S ACTIVITY

Individually, make a list of things you want to start praying about together. Start with specifics regarding your marriage and move from there to extended families, church matters, neighborhood and local concerns, world events, and anything else that comes to mind. Share your concerns with one another (many are likely to overlap) and pray for all you can reasonably concentrate on today. Keep your lists where you'll see them (and add to them) regularly and pray more frequently for those things until God answers.

Prayer not only draws you closer to God, but it's the key experience in keeping your marriage relationship close and alive.
@pastorjoecyr

FORTY-FOUR

ADJUST YOUR VOLUME CONTROL

Avoid both the silent treatment and the loud treatment.

Have you ever had a radio, television, or other piece of electronic equipment with a faulty volume control? It's too soft to hear, so you adjust the volume ever so slightly and SUDDENLY IT'S LOUD ENOUGH TO DEAFEN YOUR NEIGHBORS!

A lot of marriages are like that. I said, A LOT OF MARRIAGES ARE LIKE THAT! Conflicts and disagreements are going to occur when two people combine their lives, preferences, and habits. The key is not only to resolve conflict quickly but to resolve it in a healthy way. But couples can go wrong in extremely different ways.

Some people operate at one end of the spectrum with The Silent Treatment. Everyone has seen The Silent Treatment; most have used it! In The Silent Treatment, you sit and keep quiet. If the other person asks what's wrong, you say "Nothing," even though it's obvious something is.

Other people go to the opposite extreme with The Loud Treatment. Yelling is their solution for everything. They shout to add intensity to what they're saying. They may "win" an argument through intimidation, but they damage the relationship.

Both The Silent Treatment and The Loud Treatment are bad ways to communicate. They're immature ways of saying:

"I don't want to talk to you."

"I don't care enough to deal with the issues."

"I'm mad and want you to know it."

"I insist on getting my way."

If you can't control your temper, it's a spiritual problem. Instead of shutting down or venting your frustrations on your spouse, work it out with God. Silently ask Him to forgive you and pray for His will to come through loud and clear.

THOUGHT FOR THE DAY

"A gentle answer turns away wrath, but a harsh word stirs up anger" (Proverbs 15:1).

TODAY'S ACTIVITY

Today you need to be brutally honest with one another, both to confess any past incidents of either The Silent Treatment or The Loud Treatment, and to point out examples your spouse might not see in himself or herself. Agree that from now on, in an argument, you both have the right to ask politely, "May we adjust the volume control before we continue?" After you've shared with one another, ask God to work in both your lives to minimize the number of your conflicts as well as their intensity.

Practice verbal intimacy. When you disagree, don't do it from across the house. Being eye-to-eye can turn down the heat.
@ryandarrow

FORTY-FIVE

ANOTHER CRISIS? HA!

Laugh at challenges and disappointments.

When you first start out in life together, lots of things seem bigger and more urgent than they really are. You forget to pay a bill and get a threatening letter from the utility company? Don't panic; just write the check. An emergency dental procedure causes you to miss an important meeting at work? Happens to everyone sometimes; your boss will understand. You're half an hour late picking up a friend at the airport as you promised? Explain why and ask forgiveness; that's what friends are for.

Things *will* go wrong in life, and sometimes those things will be embarrassing, regrettable, or even painful. Just focus most of your time and energy into remedying the problem and not so much in wondering what other people must think about you.

In fact, try to learn to laugh in the face of adversity. Search for the joy and humor in every situation. Also look around for friends and family members who demonstrate the ability to endure the worst life can throw at them with very little trauma (or drama). Right now I'm thinking about Jim and Betty Rodgers, two close friends who are facing adversity that would quickly defeat many other people. Instead, they are laughing their way through the storm. Look for similar examples among people you know, and don't let anything or anyone steal your joy!

If you learn to laugh at life's mishaps, you'll turn disappointments and even potential disasters into precious shared stories.

THOUGHT FOR THE DAY

"A hot-tempered person stirs up conflict, but the one who is patient calms a quarrel" (Proverbs 15:18).

TODAY'S ACTIVITY

Start a conversation today about people you know who model a consistent positive attitude throughout the difficulties in life. Make a list. If you know the people well enough, invite them over (one at a time) or ask to visit and interview them about what makes them different. What's their secret? Were they always this way, or did they have a turning point in life? Gather as much information as you can, and then start your own tradition of laughing at the problems of life.

If you don't overreact, keep smiling, and laugh at your mistakes, you'll discover this crisis isn't that big of a deal.
@randyjumper

FORTY-SIX

SOME THINGS GROW BETTER WITH AGE

Let your love show, no matter how "cheesy."

These days I never grow tired of seeing older couples display their love for one another, proudly and publicly. Have you watched an older couple interact and thought, *They're incredibly cheesy*? I admit I used to think that about couples who dressed alike or were always together, but then I gave it some more thought.

Russell and Laverne Edwards are in their eighties. Every Sunday, Russell's tie matches Laverne's dress. There's no doubt they're together and still deeply in love.

My friends David and Beth Grant are missionaries in their sixties. I serve on a board with Beth. David always brings her to the meetings. He walks up to the room with her, carrying her stuff, serving her. Beth is also an author. (Her book *Courageous Compassion* is great!) She and I were both signing books at a trade convention in Atlanta. When I walked into the exhibit hall, sure enough, there was David, taking care of Beth. Everywhere Beth goes, David goes with her.

When I was younger, I might have described Russell and Laverne, or David and Beth, as cheesy or corny. But now I have come to realize that their seasoned, enduring love is meaningful and special. Their love is only "cheesy" in the sense that it gets better with age, like a fine cheese.

Don't ever be embarrassed about displaying affection for your spouse in public. Let your love for each other show!

THOUGHT FOR THE DAY

"Is not wisdom found among the aged? Does not long life bring understanding?" (Job 12:12)

TODAY'S ACTIVITY

Take a walk through a park or a mall and look for older couples. Watch how they relate to each other and imagine what the two of you might look like when you're their age. Start now to become the attentive couple you want to become. And if you see a couple who really impress you, let them know!

Many things get better with age, and your relationship with your spouse should be one of them. #LongHaul.
@MikeBurnette

FORTY-SEVEN

BEYOND COMPARE

Tend to the grass on your side of the fence.

I'm sure you've heard the saying, "The grass is always greener on the other side of the fence." Most people can't help but compare their lives and experiences with those of other people. They might compare houses, cars, jobs, problems (or lack of), children, or any number of things, and they grow envious if someone else comes out looking better in the comparison.

One common problem for many young couples is the tendency to compare one's *spouse* with someone else's. They visit another couple to have dinner, and on the way home the guy is thinking, *Jane always looks so good, and man, can she cook! Her pies are amazing. Their house is always clean. She never gets angry or upset, and she even likes watching football. It would be wonderful to be married to her.* Meanwhile, the wife's mind is on the other husband: *Dick is always compassionate, smiling, and encouraging. He could teach my husband a few things! I bet he never goes hunting or plays golf. He probably loves working in the yard and never leaves a mess in the garage. If I had married him, my life would be so much better.*

How can the grass *not* look greener with that much manure being spread? Unfair comparisons and the resulting unrealistic expectations can create severe problems in marriages. Comparing your marriage to someone else's is a dangerous trap.

So keep your gaze on your side of the fence. Thank God every day for the wonderful spouse He has given you. When it comes down to it, that grass that looks greener usually turns out to be a bunch of weeds!

THOUGHT FOR THE DAY

"You shall not covet your neighbor's house. You shall not covet your neighbor's wife, or his male or female servant, his ox or donkey, or anything that belongs to your neighbor" (Exodus 20:17).

TODAY'S ACTIVITY

Today's devotion just screams for another shot at making a list of the things you like about your spouse as you did for Devotions 3 and 26. Take a fresh look at that wonderful, unsurpassable, unique person you married and list the things you like about them. By now you should have some new observations to add to the lists you made previously. And as usual, find a fun way to celebrate your marriage after you share your lists.

You know your worst and, typically, only see someone else's best. Comparisons cannot help but be riddled with lies.
@RachelLBRoss

FORTY-EIGHT

OBEY. PAY. DELAY.

Do whatever it takes to keep your finances in order.

Few things create as much stress on young couples early in marriage than money problems. Marissa Mayer, now CEO of Yahoo, once stated that credit card companies can predict with 98 percent accuracy two years in advance when a couple is going to divorce, based on the couple's spending patterns.

Debt puts a huge strain on a marriage. I'd like to suggest three simple words that will help you create a strong and healthy financial future.

The first word is *obey*. If you obey God's principles for your finances, you'll be financially healthy and will avoid much conflict. At the beginning of your marriage, make the decision to tithe, to give God the first 10 percent of your income. Tithing is a wonderful way to ensure you always put His kingdom first.

The second word is *pay*. For every purchase you need to make, large or small, think *pay now* instead of *pay later*. Pay cash for everything you buy. Don't use credit cards at all. If you don't have the money, don't make the purchase.

That leads to the third word: *delay*. When you spend what you don't have, you engage in what the government calls "deficit spending." In other words, you accumulate debt—the number one enemy of financial health and a threat to your marriage. Here's a great phrase to memorize and say often: "I'm sorry. We can't afford that."

Faithful obedience leads to blessing and is the foundation for financial freedom. Try it. Then watch and see how God will bless you.

THOUGHT FOR THE DAY

"Do not worry, saying 'What shall we eat?' or 'What shall we drink?' or 'What shall we wear?' . . . But seek first [God's] kingdom and his righteousness, and all these things will be given to you as well" (Matthew 6:31, 33).

TODAY'S ACTIVITY

If you and your spouse haven't yet had a heart-to-heart about your finances, don't put it off any longer. You have different financial backgrounds, thoughts, ideas, discipline, and style, so combine your strengths and reach an agreement. Sit down today and determine: How much do you spend? How much do you save? Who decides? What's reasonable? For which of your needs should you pay now, and which can be delayed? And throughout it all, are you being obedient to God?

Don't become prey to unwise financial management. Make a plan for giving, spending, and saving.
@RyanPMoore

FORTY-NINE

FIGHT FAIR.

There's a right way and a wrong way to argue.

Conflict is a part of every marriage . . . a regular part. No matter how much you focus on peace and harmony, you'll still disagree. But you can keep your arguments from escalating by determining ahead of time what you will and won't say to one another. Decide together things you'll never say in an argument.

You might start with these:

"Divorce." Don't ever let that word come out of your mouth. If you say it once, it's easier to say the next time. Threatening to end the relationship is a power play that's basically abuse. It's like saying, "I care more about this issue than I care about you." That threat will never be forgotten.

"You always . . ." or "You never . . ." Generalizations make almost any issue bigger. Eliminate all exaggeration and address specific issues directly and honestly.

Now here are some things you *can* say that will almost always be welcomed:

"I was wrong." If something was your fault and you know it, just cut right to the chase with an admission of guilt. Don't offer lame excuses or try to shift blame. Confess and move on.

"I'm sorry." Don't just admit to an offense. Tell your spouse how badly you feel about it.

"What can I do to make it right?" The conflict isn't settled until you attempt to resolve it to your spouse's satisfaction. And the best way to do that is to ask.

Apologize. Take responsibility. Offer to make amends. It's a great way to end an argument! The best argument is one that is over—forgiven and forgotten!

THOUGHT FOR THE DAY

"Godly sorrow brings repentance that leads to salvation and leaves no regret, but worldly sorrow brings death" (2 Corinthians 7:10).

TODAY'S ACTIVITY

Today's devotional should have gotten you started, but go ahead and take it from there. First work together to construct a list of words and phrases that you agree to ban from all further arguments. Then add to the list things that you *would* like to hear. Even better, discuss how the two of you might keep conflict to a minimum from this point forward.

Predetermined ground rules prevent heartache and prepare for success.
@Aaron_Hlavin

FIFTY

SAFE AND SURROUNDED

Be accountable to one another.

No one goes into marriage planning to have an affair or get a divorce. So why do so many marriages fail? I'm convinced it's because couples never put safeguards in place. They foolishly believe it could never happen to them, but no one is immune from moral failure.

Temptation is strongest when a person is isolated. People tend to act out of character when they don't have to answer to anyone or have no fear of being caught. So if you or your spouse resists accountability, that's a big red flag.

One of the best ways to avoid failure is to be accountable to your spouse at all times. I intentionally surround myself with people and accountability systems so if I'm tempted, I have someone who cares enough to confront me before I do wrong. For example:

Two pastors on our staff have my social media and computer passwords.

My email is automatically copied to Cindy's computer at home.

Virtually everyone has the passcode to unlock my phone.

I don't travel alone.

I avoid privacy and embrace accountability.

In addition, here are a few things everyone can do to increase accountability:

Share passwords, including computer, Facebook, and phone unlock codes.

Install filtering and monitoring software on your Internet service provider and give your spouse access.

Schedule an annual marriage checkup with your pastor or a counselor.

Empower a trusted friend to ask tough questions at any time.

Offer information before your spouse needs to ask.

Choosing to be accountable isn't always convenient, but it's much easier to avoid a problem now than to try to fix one later.

THOUGHT FOR THE DAY

"If you think you are standing firm, be careful that you don't fall!" (1 Corinthians 10:12)

TODAY'S ACTIVITY

Verbally commit to be accountable to one another—forever. Then use the previous suggestions to create a plan with specific steps to ensure that neither of you is ever left in isolation and given the opportunity to yield to moral temptations.

Get naked! Be authentic! If you're the only one who knows your secrets, you're in trouble. Give others total access.
@andrewtempleton

FIFTY-ONE

MAKE TIME FOR WHAT'S IMPORTANT

Determine, then defend, your priorities.

In the 1960s, a number of time-management experts testified before a Senate sub-committee. Because of new and better technology, they predicted that within twenty years people would work far fewer hours each week and fewer weeks each year. Retirement would come earlier, and the greatest challenge would be filling all our newfound free time. Didn't exactly work out that way, did it?

Today we actually brag about our busyness, how many hours we work, how little we sleep, and our ability to multitask. We're too busy for the things that should matter most—including marriage. If couples don't quickly *determine* and *defend* their priorities, then society, work, and others will determine them instead.

After determining your priorities, here are a few ways to defend them:

Block family time on your calendar. Schedule an evening together like you would any other appointment.

Learn to say no. Other options (even good ones) will attempt to lure you away from your priorities. Be spontaneous when you can, but say no when you need to.

Turn off your phones. You can be at the same place with your spouse, but not really be together! Put away the phones and rediscover conversation.

Slow down. It sounds simple, but it's not. Take time for each other. Walk the dog. Sit on the porch. Go to bed early. Don't be in such a hurry!

Put God first. When you put God first in your schedule, He protects and blesses your time. When you don't, you'll never achieve a proper balance.

Give these matters some thought, and we'll continue along the same lines in the following devotion.

THOUGHT FOR THE DAY

"Come to me, all you who are weary and burdened, and I will give you rest. Take my yoke upon you and learn from me, for I am gentle and humble in heart, and you will find rest for your souls. For my yoke is easy and my burden is light" (Matthew 11:28–30).

TODAY'S ACTIVITY

You've probably discussed priorities for your marriage, but today be as specific as possible. Make a list of everything that's important to you as a couple. Take your time. When finished, prioritize the items on the list. Keep your list handy (and keep thinking about what you might want to add or change) for the next devotional.

Essential in a long-lasting marriage is a commitment to Sabbath together. Fight for it. Perfect rest leads to fruitful work.
@NathanKollar

FIFTY-TWO

YOUR BIG PICTURE

Keep your focus on what you feel is most important for your family.

Six months before Cindy and I got married, I bought my first almost-new car. I gave it to Cindy to drive, and I took hers. One afternoon, Cindy came into my office, crying. When I asked what was wrong, she just took her hand from behind her back and held up a piece of my new car. She had hit another car in the parking lot. I wasn't happy my car was wrecked, but I hugged her and said, "Cars come and go. You are what matters to me."

The big picture of a person's life is his or her top priority. The big picture for me at that point of life was marrying the beautiful girl I loved.

Keep the big picture of your marriage in mind at all times. The changes and surprises of life won't cause enormous stress if you stay focused on what really matters.

A big-picture focus helps you cope with minor frustrations. It will keep you from overreacting when things break, plants die, freezers don't freeze, stuff gets spilled, and tires go flat.

A big-picture focus also helps you prioritize. I once showed up unexpectedly at Tyler's ninth-grade classroom to sign him out of English class so he could join me for lunch with a missionary from the Congo. We spent an hour listening to stories and crying about lost and hurting people. It was a big-picture decision that we both still remember.

Years ago I determined that the big picture for my home is for every member of my family to be a lifelong follower of Jesus. Compared to that, nothing else matters—not ruined plans . . . and not even wrecked cars!

THOUGHT FOR THE DAY

"'Love the Lord your God with all your heart and with all your soul and with all your mind.' This is the first and greatest commandment. And the second is like it: 'Love your neighbor as yourself'" (Matthew 22:37–39).

TODAY'S ACTIVITY

Retrieve the list you made after the previous devotion. Review the priorities you named and discuss what you want to be the big picture for your marriage. What is the one crucial priority that supersedes all the others? (After you determine your big picture, you may need to make adjustments in how you spend your time, invest your money, etc.)

**Panorama priorities trump life's urgencies.
Pray for the mind of Christ, vision of God,
and Spirit-empowered courage. #clarity**
@Jennifer_McAfee

FIFTY-THREE

HOME IMPROVEMENT

Set high standards.

Suppose you want to build a house and you have a choice between two contractors. The first one tells you, "We can save you some money because we cut some corners with substandard plumbing and use electricians who aren't union certified, but I think the work will hold up fine . . . for a while. All in all, we do just as good a job as most anybody else."

The second contractor looks you in the eye and says, "For the past twenty years our company has been rated the best in the state. We take a little longer than average and we might cost a bit more, but you'll have solid materials and workmanship from the foundation of the home to the top of the weathervane. We guarantee everything we do."

So which one do you choose? Most people definitely want the best when building a house, yet they set considerably lower standards when building a home . . . a marriage. I hate to hear couples tell me, "We're doing as well as anyone else." Since when is that the goal!

Marriage is an institution designed by God. You and your spouse belong to Him. He has brought you together to be His instruments in this world. Your marriage is sacred and holy. You are loved and accepted by the Creator of the universe. Nothing about that is average!

Live and treat one another as if you are special, because you are. Keep your standards high, and the home you have created together will stand firm and endure any storm.

THOUGHT FOR THE DAY

"You are the ones chosen by God, chosen for the high calling of priestly work, chosen to be a holy people, God's instruments to do his work and speak out for him, to tell others of the night-and-day difference he made for you—from nothing to something, from rejected to accepted" (1 Peter 2:9–10, *Message*).

TODAY'S ACTIVITY

Discuss with your spouse: Do you feel special? Why or why not? Do you think we are satisfied to rate our marriage "as good as most other people are doing"? If not, what standards do we want to maintain to ensure that we continually honor God with our marriage?

Your marriage needs to be one of the highest priorities. Success will only come when you keep it at the forefront.
@pastorjoecyr

FIFTY-FOUR

CHECK THE PACE OF YOUR RACE

Establish a sustainable pace.

Perhaps you've heard people speak of "running the race" in reference to going through life, and many times the phrase refers specifically to the Christian life. (The "rat race" is another, more secular reference.) But runners might question the phrase. Exactly what kind of running are you referring to?

Sprinters work to establish speed. They know that tenths of seconds (or even hundredths of seconds) can make the difference between winning and losing. They go all out, from the sound of the gun. They race for the finish line and cross with no energy left. Many times you'll see them fall to the ground, exhausted.

Distance runners have a different strategy. They train for marathons (and even longer distances). Attempting to sprint from start to finish of a 26.2-mile route would be foolish, and even dangerous to the person's health. So marathoners try to establish a sustainable pace that pushes their endurance, yet gets them to the finish line.

Your marriage is not a sprint. By now, you may have discovered as much. Many couples are a bit too ambitious as they start their lives together and eventually learn through trial and error what pace of life works best for them.

If you haven't yet done so, find a sustainable pace that allows your relationship to progress, because marriage (and life) is a marathon. Push too hard, and you burn out. Go too slow, and you stagnate and risk not finishing. Find the pace that works so you can cross the line together. That way, you're both winners!

THOUGHT FOR THE DAY

"Do you not know that in a race all the runners run, but only one gets the prize? Run in such a way as to get the prize" (1 Corinthians 9:24).

TODAY'S ACTIVITY

Consider that since your marriage is a marathon, you probably haven't reached the .2-mile point yet, much less the twenty-six miles that are beyond. With that in mind, discuss with your spouse: How are we trying to sprint when we should be slowing down a bit? In what areas do we need to pick up the pace in order to reach the finish line in reasonable time? What specifically would a sustainable pace look like in our marriage?

Don't ever give up seeing the best in one another. Let a passionate pursuit of a positive perspective be your daily goal.
@ryandarrow

FIFTY-FIVE

JUST DESSERTS?

Be thankful you don't get what you deserve.

Occasionally you might hear of someone getting his "just desserts," meaning he is receiving what he truly has coming to him. How about you: Would *you* like to receive everything you deserve?

I hear comments along those lines all the time, especially from people who have only been married a short while:

"I deserve someone who treats me better."

"I deserve a husband who makes more money."

"I deserve a wife who is more affectionate."

"I deserve [you name it]."

When I hear such comments I cringe, because those are toxic thoughts in a marriage. To begin with, the phrase presumes there's little if anything wrong with *you*. If you *deserve* to be treated better, does that mean you never mistreat the other person? It's a not-so-subtle way of passing judgment.

In addition, "I deserve" voices dissatisfaction with your spouse and compares that person to a fantasy that doesn't exist. If you found someone who made more money, they would certainly have other shortcomings. If you had someone more affectionate, you would likely discover other issues very quickly.

Finally, you had better be perfect if you ask for all you deserve because if you've ever sinned, you deserve death. Thankfully, our merciful God offers the gift of eternal life instead! Be grateful God doesn't give us our just deserts!

The next time you're tempted to think, *I deserve . . .*, think instead about becoming the person your spouse deserves. Because if you ever find that perfect someone you think you "deserve," that person would certainly deserve better than you!

THOUGHT FOR THE DAY

"But now apart from the law the righteousness of God has been made known. . . . This righteousness is given through faith in Jesus Christ to all who believe. There is no difference between Jew and Gentile, for all have sinned and fall short of the glory of God, and all are justified freely by his grace through the redemption that came by Christ Jesus" (Romans 3:21–24).

TODAY'S ACTIVITY

To ensure that you step away from an "I deserve" mentality, spend some time today writing a poem, song, or essay for your spouse. The title should be, "You Deserve . . ."

Your spouse deserves love, mercy, and joy.
You deserve the opportunity to give them
those things. Get what you both deserve!
@randyjumper

FIFTY-SIX

STRETCH YOURSELF

Be flexible!

I've discovered that if I want to avoid back pain, I have to stay flexible, so I do a lot of stretching to keep feeling good. I stretch twenty-five minutes every morning and twenty-five minutes every night. (My family is sick of hearing the "Beep! Beep!" of my stretch timer!)

Similarly, young couples who want to avoid unnecessary pain in their marriage need to learn to be flexible! A flexible person understands, "I'm not always going to get my way. I've got to be open to different things." That means flexibility is a choice. You demonstrate flexibility when you choose to put your spouse first, when you choose not to insist on your opinion, or when you hit any of life's numerous speed bumps with a smile.

Flexible couples thrive in uncertain times, because they adapt to unexpected circumstances. They don't overreact to change. Instead of freaking out, they go with the flow. As a result, they sometimes discover joy in unexpected places.

When I used to drive Parker to junior high school, I wanted to expose him to all kinds of music. We agreed to take turns choosing what we would listen to, alternating days. It became an exercise in flexibility for both of us! The effort really paid off one morning as we listened to classical music. Parker said, "Wow, Dad! Did you hear that viola?" I was a proud father! Of course, the next day we listened to Radio Disney and it was my turn to be flexible.

The "stretch timer" in marriage has no "Off" setting. You always need to be flexible. When you try something new, you will discover new joys and blessings in life.

THOUGHT FOR THE DAY

"Finally, be strong in the Lord and in his mighty power. Put on the full armor of God, so that you can take your stand against the devil's schemes" (Ephesians 6:10–11).

TODAY'S ACTIVITY

Think back across your marriage so far. Using a scale of 1 (least) to 10 (most), rate your flexibility in each of the following categories. First do this independently, and then share and discuss your responses with your spouse.

Financial matters

Dealing with in-laws and other family members

Social interaction with friends

Spiritual development

And for extra credit, how would you rate you and your spouse on your mutual flexibility?

One trait of healthy marriage is a couple who are mutually submitted to each other. Stop snapping & start bending.
@MikeBurnette

FIFTY-SEVEN

THE VOW IS FOR NOW

Commit to one another—no matter what.

All young lovers who recite marriage vows to one another know they're making a commitment. What many don't seem to realize, however, is that the vow is not just a one-time recitation, but a lifelong covenant. The commitment you expressed on your wedding day should be reiterated—and demonstrated—every day thereafter.

Sadly, commitment is fast becoming a disposable commodity in our society. When difficulties come along in marriage (and they do, all too often), some people are quick to bail out. The vow they took—that so-called *commitment*—is easily disregarded.

The terms of a commitment are "no matter what," and I challenge you to develop a no-matter-what mentality for everything you vowed to one another at your wedding ceremony. That includes phases of life when you are poor . . . when you are sick . . . when you're seeing a lot more of the "worse" side of life than the "better." Those circumstances don't negate the fact that you've made a commitment to one another.

Commitment isn't contingent on conditions; it's ultimately a choice. I choose to love Cindy. Does she irritate me sometimes? Absolutely! I may possibly have irritated her once or twice. We've had good times (when commitment is automatic) and bad times (when we chose to be committed). At all times my commitment is a choice I make and one I will honor.

Commitment is proven through actions, not words. Your marriage vows shouldn't be taken lightly. They are a commitment, intended to last for a lifetime.

THOUGHT FOR THE DAY

"When a man makes a vow to the Lord or takes an oath to obligate himself by a pledge, he must not break his word but must do everything he said" (Numbers 30:2).

TODAY'S ACTIVITY

Compile a list of survey questions you might ask others about commitment: "How would you define commitment?" "At what point in your marriage did commitment come easiest?" "When has it been hardest?" After writing your questions, make a list of people you could ask from church, your workplace, etc. Choose people at different stages of marriage who will be honest with you. See what others can advise to help you at this early stage of your own commitment to each other.

Vows create covenants. Covenants are not heavy loads that have to be endured, covenants make difficulty endurable.
@RachelLBRoss

FIFTY-EIGHT

SOMEWHERE BETWEEN MEMORIES AND DREAMS

Celebrate good memories, but anticipate better tomorrows.

One of the great joys of my life is looking back over my twenty-seven years of marriage. I cheer as I see how Cindy and I have made it through numerous struggles. I still tear up when I think of the births of our two sons. I laugh at so many memories I carry.

Yet an equally great joy, and probably even greater, is looking ahead. By this point in my life I've learned that even though I *think* I know what I can expect, I may be completely wrong. Some of life's most unplanned, unexpected surprises have become the memories I recall with the most fondness.

So as you move along in your marriage, look over your shoulder occasionally to remember and cherish the special moments you've had so far. But most of the time, keep your eyes on the road ahead with eager anticipation. Your life holds . . . well, I can't tell you what it holds, and that's the point I'm trying to make.

Recently, I was in Hong Kong and was thirteen hours ahead of my time zone in North Little Rock. By noon in Arkansas, it's the next day in Hong Kong! I would be away for my younger son's birthday, so I sent him a text to tell him, "You're going to love tomorrow! Your birthday is great. I've already seen it, and it's wonderful!"

Celebrate the memories of the past even as you leave the hurts and pain behind, because yesterday is gone. Cherish today as a gift from God . . . and anticipate tomorrow. God has great things in store for you. I pray you follow God in a lifetime of obedience and enjoy His richest blessings.

THOUGHT FOR THE DAY

"Jesus Christ is the same yesterday and today and forever" (Hebrews 13:8).

TODAY'S ACTIVITY

Spend some time looking ahead together. Tell one another the story of your life if you had the opportunity to write it. Where will you be in five years? In fifteen? In fifty? What would you accomplish? When you finish, you might want to jot down the high points and put them somewhere that will serve as a "time capsule" (family Bible, safety deposit box, etc.). At some distant future point, see if your actual life doesn't surpass what you would have planned for yourselves.

Memories are made spontaneously, but they're also planned intentionally. Dream together about future memories.
@RyanPMoore

FIFTY-NINE

A LITTLE BODY WORK

Find your unique balance as a couple.

People tend to think of themselves in one of two ways. Some people seem to proclaim, "I'm strong and you're weak. If you had more of my wonderful strength, the world (or our marriage) would be a better place!"

Others have the opposite perspective. "I'm weak and you're strong. I have nothing to contribute on my own. People like me are the real problem in the world (or in our marriage)."

Paul wrote about the "body of Christ" in Romans 12. He explained that in the human body, every part is important. Every part is necessary. If one part stops functioning, the entire body is affected.

You may be familiar with this teaching and the usual spiritual applications that are made—believers need one another, no matter how strong or weak, and only by working together can we operate effectively.

However, I want you to think about the same content in the context of your marriage. What strengths does your spouse bring to the relationship? If you had never met your spouse, would your life be as complete?

Every person has a special, unique, God-ordained purpose. When believers get together and combine their gifts, the church gets stronger. Whenever you and your spouse begin to identify and develop your strengths, you can accomplish God's plan and purpose for your marriage and your family.

Different personalities and strengths create a unique balance. Find that balance in your marriage and see how God will use it for His glory!

THOUGHT FOR THE DAY

"Just as a body, though one, has many parts, but all its many parts form one body, so it is with Christ. . . . God has put the body together, giving greater honor to the parts that lacked it, so that there should be no division in the body, but that its parts should have equal concern for each other" (1 Corinthians 12:12, 24–25).

TODAY'S ACTIVITY

Try to determine your personal strengths, especially in regard to your marriage, in terms of various body parts. For example, the spouse who runs most of the errands might be the "feet" or if it's a 50/50 situation, you each might be a "foot." After you write down all the body parts you think apply to you, see if your spouse agrees. Then check to see if any crucial body parts are missing and see if you can think harder to fill in the missing parts.

A successful marriage is a mutually beneficial partnership, balanced and loving, which at its core is sacrificial.
@Aaron_Hlavin

SIXTY

HOME IS WHERE THE BEARS AREN'T

Make your home a secure place.

Many years ago, I went camping. I spent the night in a tent, in the really scary wilderness of a state park. I would like to say I *slept* in a tent, but truth be told, I spent the entire night lying awake, wondering when a huge bear would rip through the flimsy nylon surrounding me and eat me for breakfast. That was more than twenty years ago, and it was the last time I went tent camping. During that long, long night, I found out something about myself: I like walls.

Without walls, there's nothing to keep out intruders . . . a house is vulnerable to every little gust of wind, much less a storm . . . you don't feel safe and secure.

Your home is under constant attack from the media onslaught of sexual innuendo, the vices and temptations that are only one click away on the Internet, and special interest groups that are attempting to redefine *marriage* and *family*. But in the midst of the chaos and danger, your home can be a safe and secure place—if you construct the right walls.

Build a wall of *prayer*. Build a wall of *purity*. Build a wall of *dedication to God*. Keep those walls repaired and always strong. Know they will protect you when you take bold risks, struggle, and make mistakes. They will keep you secure as you love, share dreams, and grow as individuals and a couple. Always be grateful that your home is a place where you are safe from enemies and protected from storms, a place that keeps you together.

THOUGHT FOR THE DAY

"No longer will violence be heard in your land, nor ruin or destruction within your borders, but you will call your walls Salvation and your gates Praise" (Isaiah 60:18).

TODAY'S ACTIVITY

You were given three "walls" to consider to get you started (prayer, purity, and dedication to God), but a strong house can use more. Spend your together time today listing other foundational walls you want to establish that will keep your family safe and secure.

Even Superman has a fortress to retreat to so he can recharge. Create a home of peace—the real blessing is at home.
@andrewtempleton

SIXTY-ONE

THE WHOLE TRUTH, AND NOTHING BUT THE TRUTH

Quit making excuses for not telling the truth.

When Parker was four years old he took Cindy's wedding ring off the bathroom counter. She didn't want to upset me when she couldn't find it, so she didn't tell me it was missing. But soon I got a call from our insurance company asking about the claim I had submitted, and there was a little tension in our house that night!

One crucial key to a solid, lasting marriage is truth telling, although a spouse may have any number of reasons to lie to the other. For example:

Shame—truth requires admitting faults, which can make someone feel ashamed. It's easier to keep quiet or create a lie.

Habit—some people have told lies for so long, they do it without thinking. Lying has become an addiction.

Concealment—when people are desperate to keep a secret hidden, they will lie (and do anything else).

Insecurity—if someone is afraid to admit how much another person matters, he or she may deny such feelings by lying about various positive truths (strong feelings of love, admiration, need, etc.).

Fear—many people live a perpetual lie because they fear that if a spouse really knew the truth about them, he or she wouldn't love them anymore.

By the way, on the suggestion of our friend Johanna we gave Parker another ring and secretly followed him. He put it in the tubing of our exercise bike. When we checked, sure enough, the wedding ring was there as well.

So resolve to tell each other the truth always and to not allow secrets in your marriage. You'll be fully known and fully loved . . . and you'll prevent a lot of problems along the way.

THOUGHT FOR THE DAY

"Love does not delight in evil but rejoices with the truth" (1 Corinthians 13:6).

TODAY'S ACTIVITY

Complete honesty can be hard, but this is the day to be totally truthful with your spouse. If you've been keeping a secret, or have been insecure or fearful, the sooner you get the truth out in the open, the better. And even if you've only been telling "little white lies," confess them and clear the slate (unless it's something like surprising him or her with a great gift).

Make an intentional commitment to be honest in your marriage or deception will creep in and build wedges between you.
@NathanKollar

SIXTY-TWO

O–L–L–L–L–D FRIENDS

Expect your friendships to get stronger with time.

At Tyler's wedding, I was shocked to see Kurt and Martha, my first babysitters and dear friends of my parents for fifty years! When I was just a little guy, they were the only people I would stay with. My parents didn't even know Kurt and Martha were coming. They decided to surprise us all.

Young couples rarely look that far ahead, yet it's awesome to consider that some of the friendships you form at the beginning of your marriage could become fifty-year friends! Fifty-year friends are special because they share all the key moments of your life: your marriage, the birth of your children, and all the birthdays and graduations. And they're still there for you after your children move out. Fifty-year friends are with you during the good times and the bad. As you grow old together, your friendship only deepens.

When you first start out, it's natural to spend most of your time with each other. But wise couples intentionally look for acquaintances who just might become fifty-year friends! They keep an eye out for other couples who:

Share their desire to be lifelong followers of Jesus;

Are fun to spend time with;

Aren't afraid to challenge their friends to be better;

Can be trusted with whatever they are told in confidence;

Celebrate others' victories;

Are empathetic in times of struggle; and

Earnestly support their friends in prayer.

Start your search now. Fifty-year friends start as one-year friends!

THOUGHT FOR THE DAY

"One who has unreliable friends soon comes to ruin, but there is a friend who sticks closer than a brother" (Proverbs 18:24).

TODAY'S ACTIVITY

Discuss whether you and your spouse detect any potential fifty-year friends. Start with the people you already spend time with, but don't stop there. Consider each other's friends, casual acquaintances, and even people you don't know well, yet whom you respect. Think of those you know at church, work, in the neighborhood, or anywhere else you can think of. When you have identified a few couples, initiate some interaction and see if anything develops.

Fifty-year friends are a marriage must-have. The best part . . . the friendships get better with time! #LIFEtimePARTYtime
@Jennifer_McAfee

SIXTY-THREE

STORMPROOF!

Build your life and marriage on a firm foundation.

"The wise man built his house upon the rock."

Do you remember the children's song? And the Bible story on which it was based?

Jesus' parable in Matthew 7:24–27 illustrates an important truth: anything built without a solid foundation isn't likely to survive storms. That's especially true for marriage. Here are some keys for building a strong foundation:

Acknowledge your need for God. Don't be proud or foolish.

Attend church together. A good church provides an environment not only to worship and learn, but also to laugh, cry, study, and otherwise interact with others. With all the challenges in our society today, we need church more than ever.

Pray together. A regular devotion time is important, but it's only a start. Make prayer a normal, everyday occurrence in your home.

Thank God together. It reminds you that He is the source of all good things and acknowledges His lordship. It also shows others that you are dependent on Him.

Practice biblical principles. When faced with a dilemma, ask: "What does the Bible say we should do in this situation? Let's see if we can find God's answer."

Talk about God. When you talk about God, your relationship will have more depth and you'll share spiritual breakthroughs together. It may be awkward at first, but soon it will become natural.

Make Jesus the center of your home. Otherwise your life will never find a satisfying balance.

You choose what matters most in your home. But if you don't start by choosing a strong foundation, nothing else will last. The wise couple builds their house upon the Rock.

THOUGHT FOR THE DAY

"Everyone who hears these words of mine and puts them into practice is like a wise man who built his house on the rock. The rain came down, the streams rose, and the winds blew and beat against that house; yet it did not fall, because it had its foundation on the rock" (Matthew 7:24–25).

TODAY'S ACTIVITY

How strong would you rate your home's current foundation, on a scale of 1 (weakest) to 10 (strongest)? Discuss with your spouse how you might make it stronger in the weeks to come. What are you not doing that you should be doing? Are you doing anything that you shouldn't?

In order for your marriage to be strong, stand strong, and last forever, build your marriage on the truth of God's Word!
@pastorjoecyr

SIXTY-FOUR

A CLEAR CONNECTION

Be slow to speak and quick to listen.

I like to watch people, and I'm always amused to see someone on a cell phone with a bad connection, yelling to be heard. I want to interrupt and explain that volume is not the problem. It's that the two parties are not properly connected.

A recent study showed that the average family spends just fourteen and a half minutes a day talking to each other. And it seems that when we *are* talking, we're saying things like, "You haven't heard a word I've said!" or "Why aren't you listening to me?" When we don't set aside adequate time to make a connection, it's no wonder our communication suffers.

The same principle holds true for your marriage. When husband and wife don't share a strong connection, communication suffers. Thankfully, there's a good solution that will ensure clear connection, and it's something anyone can do: *listen!*

Be a better listener during conversations. Pay careful attention to what your spouse is saying rather than prematurely preparing your response. Simply try to understand what the other person is thinking and feeling. Don't just listen for words; listen for feelings. Then, after listening, but before replying, think about what you're going to say and how to say it. Don't just pop off with the first thing that comes to your mind.

Maybe you remember those cell phone commercials where a guy walked around with a phone to his ear, asking: "Can you hear me now?" The point was that when the connection is clear, communication is much better. And that's exactly the point I hope you and your spouse will always remember.

THOUGHT FOR THE DAY

"My dear brothers and sisters, take note of this: Everyone should be quick to listen, slow to speak and slow to become angry, because human anger does not produce the righteousness that God desires" (James 1:19–20).

TODAY'S ACTIVITY

Plan some listening exercises. Perhaps you want to practice with one another, but you might benefit more by hanging around with whichever of your friends always seems to monopolize conversations. Practice listening to him or her without interrupting or mentally rolling your eyes. Ask follow-up questions to show involvement. Your mind may drift at first or you might have to feign interest, but in time your listening skills will become much stronger.

The best form of communication involves a speaker and a listener. One of you will have to pipe down and listen up!
@ryandarrow

SIXTY-FIVE

HOW TO WEAKEN YOUR MARRIAGE

Avoid common habits that intensify conflicts.

All marriages will undergo conflict. Couples will disagree. That's perfectly normal. But when that happens, there are some almost surefire things you can do to make the situation worse.

Share the problem with other people first. Nobody wants to hear about a problem secondhand. Tell your spouse first—not parents, friends, etc.

Generalize. Comments such as, "You always gripe at me," or "You never take me anywhere" only give your spouse a chance to quickly prove you wrong and sidetrack the conversation from the issue at hand.

Exaggerate. (For example, "I'm never talking to you again.") Stick to the facts to avoid inflaming arguments.

Walk out. Physically walking away or mentally checking out of the conversation are equally fruitless. Ask for a brief timeout if you need one, but then resume the discussion and resolve the problem.

Threaten to end the relationship. Such threats might end the argument, but you lose trust and integrity (and possibly the relationship) as a result.

Clam up. Keeping silent or pretending the problem doesn't exist won't help. Time doesn't heal all wounds. Resolution and healing require mutual honesty and effort.

Assume motives. Maybe he wasn't ignoring you; he might not have heard you. Maybe she wasn't lying to you but only made an honest mistake. Check the facts before making potentially destructive presumptions.

Refuse help. Drowning people and distraught couples shouldn't wait too long to yell for help. When you can't resolve a conflict on your own, ask a trusted friend or pastor to sit down with you and help facilitate communication.

If you can avoid these pitfalls that make conflict worse, your marriage will be back on track much, much quicker.

THOUGHT FOR THE DAY

"Do not repay anyone evil for evil. Be careful to do what is right in the eyes of everyone" (Romans 12:17).

TODAY'S ACTIVITY

By this point in your marriage, you've probably had a number of conflicts already. Are you guilty of any of the improper responses mentioned in today's devotion? If so, select one or two specific examples and "redo" them. Discuss with your spouse how you *should* have handled the disagreement so that next time something similar occurs, you'll be ready with a more constructive response.

Learn to manage conflict biblically, not selfishly. Your habits during conflict determine whether your marriage will last.
@randyjumper

SIXTY-SIX

GOAL SHARING

Set goals for all aspects of your marriage.

When you were single, you set your own goals. Perhaps at the top of the list was to fall in love and get married! Now that you're married, it's just as important to set goals, yet it can be challenging to do so together. Your mutual goals will help you stay focused and disciplined. Otherwise you have a tendency to make decisions based on the emotion of the moment, and may later regret your action. I suggest you start with the following goals:

Financial—This category includes giving (How much to God? How much to other good causes? Etc.), saving (both short-term and long-term goals), and debt reduction (because debt is dangerous to a marriage). Plan for buying a home, establishing college funds for kids, retirement, etc.

Future—What do you want to accomplish as a couple in ministry, business, etc.? What would you like to do for others? What do you want the impact of your life to be?

Spiritual Growth—Set some goals for Bible reading, church attendance, prayer, and ministry involvement.

Fun—Where do you want to go on vacation? What's the best way to spend an unexpected day off work? What "big thing" would you like to do together? You may not be able to afford anything major right now, but you can have fun planning and saving for it!

Going through life without set goals is like running a race without knowing the direction of the finish line. But when you have definable goals, you can celebrate progress along the way until the day you actually reach them!

THOUGHT FOR THE DAY

"I press on toward the goal to win the prize for which God has called me heavenward in Christ Jesus" (Philippians 3:14).

TODAY'S ACTIVITY

You've done some planning and goal setting for other devotional activities, but spend time today updating your plans and ensuring that you are including all areas of your marriage. This time be as specific as possible with dates, details, etc.

Most couples start with similar short-term goals in mind. Spend time developing your long-term strategies too.
@MikeBurnette

SIXTY-SEVEN

MARRIAGE CHECKUP

*Regularly examine your marriage objectively
for signs of weakness.*

At a doctor's office you start by filling out a lot of paperwork. One of the forms is always a list of symptoms. You're supposed to check any that apply to you so the doctor will have a better idea of what to check on or how to treat you. Perhaps it would be helpful to have something similar for a regular marriage checkup.

_____ 1. Do you feel unloved at times?

_____ 2. Do you feel uncomfortable at home?

_____ 3. Do bad times outnumber the good?

_____ 4. Do you feel spiritually stagnant?

_____ 5. Is there abuse (physical, verbal, or emotional) in the home?

_____ 6. Do you often leave home angry?

_____ 7. Are you emotionally or physically attached to someone other than your spouse?

_____ 8. Do you harbor resentment against someone in your family?

_____ 9. Do you sense the need to investigate your spouse?

_____ 10. Are you happier away from home than with your spouse?

_____ 11. Do you hide spending from your spouse?

_____ 12. Have you considered divorce?

_____ 13. Do you hear "I love you" less often than you used to?

_____ 14. Do you crave more intimacy with your spouse?

_____ 15. Do you feel hopeless?

I realize you just got married and probably aren't worried about these symptoms yet, but any "yes" answer is a warning sign. That's why you get doctor's checkups — to detect minor problems before they become major ones. So review these questions every six months or so as a semiannual marriage checkup!

THOUGHT FOR THE DAY

"Test me, LORD, and try me, examine my heart and my mind; for I have always been mindful of your unfailing love and have lived in reliance on your faithfulness" (Psalm 26:2–3).

TODAY'S ACTIVITY

It's early in your marriage, but go ahead and take the checkup, independent of your spouse. If neither of you have any checkmarks, you're good for now. But if you find a specific problem that needs to be addressed, work together to get help right away. If you begin to sense some concern in other areas, mark those as well for special attention in the near future.

Nothing will magnify who you truly are like marriage. It requires great courage to look at the image that emerges.
@RachelLBRoss

SIXTY-EIGHT

THE "HOW" OF FORGIVENESS

Learn to forgive, especially when forgiveness is difficult.

Forgiveness is an essential element of any relationship, especially marriage. If you want your marriage to remain healthy, it's necessary to forgive when you've been hurt or wounded. Lack of forgiveness will destroy your marriage and your home. Most people *want* to forgive. The question is "How?"

First, accept God's forgiveness. Many times it's difficult to forgive someone else because you haven't forgiven yourself. Don't be held hostage by the past. Know that God forgives you, enabling you to forgive yourself and then forgive your spouse. It's a powerful principle: forgiven people forgive people.

Second, remember we're all imperfect. When you're hurt and angry you tend to lose perspective. The fact is we're all sinners capable of hurting others intentionally.

Third, give up the right to get even. This is the heart of forgiveness. Every time you remember the hurt, forgive again.

Fourth, focus on God's plan for your marriage and home. Stop dwelling on the offense. Release and forgive your spouse. He or she will need to do the same for you soon enough.

Finally, don't hesitate to take the initial step. Don't wait for an apology. Choose to forgive.

Withholding forgiveness will erode your love. A healthy couple practices perpetual, active, ongoing forgiveness even when it isn't easy because genuine love demands it. Now that you know how, all that remains is doing it and enjoying the freedom that forgiveness will bring both of you.

THOUGHT FOR THE DAY

"Then Peter came to Jesus and asked, 'Lord, how many times shall I forgive my brother or sister who sins against me? Up to seven times?' Jesus answered, 'I tell you, not seven times, but seventy-seven times'" (Matthew 18:21–22).

TODAY'S ACTIVITY

Be aware that the person you need to forgive may not be your spouse. It could be a family member, a former friend, or someone in your past. Yet a stubborn resistance to forgive that person can affect other relationships. So discuss with your spouse any wrongdoing by those close to you that you haven't yet forgiven. Share the details with one another and pray together to prepare to forgive those longstanding offenses. If no other reason would compel you to do so, do it for the sake of your marriage.

Forgiveness is a byproduct of love.
Responding with forgiveness requires first
receiving God's forgiveness.
@RyanPMoore

SIXTY-NINE

HEAR ANY SIRENS?

Watch for warning signs of trouble.

In recent years, cities that are subject to frequent tornadoes have found that warning sirens can save a lot of lives. Whenever a tornado is approaching, the sirens give early warning and provide people time to act.

Potential marriage trouble has its own early warning signs. We need to know them, and then we need to be smart enough to respond when we detect danger. I was talking with an amazing minister in his eighties about the tragedy of so many ministers succumbing to moral temptation. He told me, "I guess I don't have to worry about it anymore. I'm too old." But then he added, "I know better than that. Anyone is capable of failure—even me."

Psychologists have identified the factors that make people most vulnerable to temptation and sexual sin. It's an easy acronym to remember: HALT, which stands for "Hungry, Angry, Lonely, and/or Tired." When people fail, one or more of those conditions is usually a factor.

I know you trust yourself and your spouse, but always assume you are capable of failing. Guard your heart and make sure you have safeguards in place! Watch carefully for your vulnerable times.

I don't plan to fail or do wrong, yet I add safeguards to ensure I do right! When I travel, I make sure Cindy or a team member travels with me.

You'll never regret safeguards. Even if you are never tempted to fail, knowing they are in place will build trust between you and your spouse.

THOUGHT FOR THE DAY

"To him who is able to keep you from stumbling and to present you before his glorious presence without fault and with great joy—to the only God our Savior be glory, majesty, power and authority, through Jesus Christ our Lord, before all ages, now and forevermore! Amen" (Jude 24).

TODAY'S ACTIVITY

Sit down with your spouse and consider how to create safeguards when needed. Start by examining both of your schedules. Are there regular times when either of you is hungry, angry, lonely, or tired? If so, start there and then move on to safeguard the rest of your schedules.

Failure to recognize a potential snare increases the possibility of entrapment. Pay close attention to your lives.
@Aaron_Hlavin

SEVENTY

A SPECIAL PRAYER FOR FAMILY

Know what is most important for your family and pray for them.

I use the acronym FAMILY as I pray for Cindy and my family. Perhaps you will find it helpful as well.

F—Followers of Jesus Christ

As my number one priority, I pray we will continue to mature by following Jesus, not going off in our own separate directions. We should be wise to the strategies of the Enemy and not easily influenced by our ever-shifting culture.

A—Active in sharing our faith

Our assignment as believers is to be the light of the world. Light penetrates darkness, so we light the world by telling others about the difference Jesus Christ makes in our lives (Matthew 5:14–16).

M—Moral purity

Our world constantly sends conflicting messages about sexual behavior. Pray that God will help you resist temptation and remain morally pure in your thoughts and actions (1 Corinthians 6:18–20).

I—Integrity

Many people have come to equate *integrity* with "telling the truth," but it's much more than that. Integrity includes choosing righteous core values and then living by them.

L—Love for people

When I pray I ask God to help us be outrageous lovers of every person He puts in our path—neighbors, lost people, critics, enemies, and even those we consider "the worst."

Y — Yielded to God

Yielding starts with being tender to God and hearing His voice, but it goes beyond hearing to include a willingness to obey.

These six qualities will strengthen the foundation of any marriage. Be sure to pray earnestly and often for those you love.

THOUGHT FOR THE DAY

"The prayer offered in faith will make the sick person well; the Lord will raise them up. If they have sinned, they will be forgiven. Therefore confess your sins to each other and pray for each other so that you may be healed. The prayer of a righteous person is powerful and effective" (James 5:15–16).

DAILY ACTIVITY

Start today with this FAMILY prayer. Use the acronym as a general outline, but add specifics to your own marriage and family as you pray. Pray for yourselves, for each other, and for other family members.

It may be awkward at first, but praying with your spouse builds the marriage, intimacy, & relationship. Plus, your spouse will love it!
@andrewtempleton

SEVENTY-ONE

THAT'S ONE WACKY FAMILY YOU'VE GOT THERE

Acknowledge weaknesses and differences in your families.

You and your spouse are both products of your upbringing, and your backgrounds may be very different. How you were parented and the atmosphere of your childhood home will have a significant impact on how you approach marriage and life together.

Cindy and I had been married more than ten years before the day we had a conversation that prompted us to recognize tendencies and traits we had brought from our respective families. It was a huge moment in our marriage! We should have talked years earlier.

It had been so simple for me to see the weaknesses in Cindy's family, but recognizing the weaknesses in my own was a much different story. Please avoid my mistake! Start with a truthful assessment of your own family; don't start by pointing out your spouse's family's weaknesses. Admit yours. You'll understand each other so much better after you honestly discuss the weaknesses and differences in your upbringing.

Consider all aspects as you discuss the differences in your upbringing: money habits (savers or spenders?), displays of affection (reserved or overly enthusiastic?), arguments (deniers, shouters, or talk-it-outers?), faith (growing, stalled, or nonexistent?), and so forth. Anywhere you discover big differences, be aware of potential conflict between you and your spouse in that area.

All families are different. It's not disloyal to admit any weaknesses in your family's approach to life. Recognizing those things and the effect they have on you is crucial to moving beyond it. The sooner you do so, the healthier your own family life will be for any future generations.

THOUGHT FOR THE DAY

"Do not remember the sins of my youth and my rebellious ways; according to your love remember me, for you, LORD, are good" (Psalm 25:7).

TODAY'S ACTIVITY

There's no better time than now to start the conversation of family upbringing, but be sure to do so prayerfully and sensitively. A new spouse may see things clearly that the other spouse has yet to acknowledge, so speak only about your own family and upbringing. Ask one another questions along the way (for clarification). And don't try to relive every childhood memory today, but make these conversations an ongoing effort.

As a slave to your own perspective, admit your shortsightedness and allow your spouse to educate you on their point of view.
@NathanKollar

SEVENTY-TWO

ADAPTING TO YOUR NEW PARENTS

Learn to love your in-laws.

When you got married, you didn't just get a spouse; you got a whole new family! And needless to say, learning to love someone else's parents can be daunting. It's also a challenge for them because overnight you replaced them as the most important person and the primary family for their son or daughter. That can be traumatic!

So keep the following things in mind as you develop and grow the important relationship with your in-laws:

Your spouse's parents will be important to him or her forever. Learning to love them is worth it!

Each of you should have difficult conversations (such as your holiday schedule) with your own parents, not your in-laws. Parents and children are used to butting heads, and then resolving it.

Be a team. Don't blame your spouse to your parents for an unpopular decision. Own the decision yourself.

Don't feel pressured to immediately call them Mom or Dad. Do what's comfortable for you.

Respect their family traditions and compromise whenever possible.

Allow your spouse to spend time alone with his or her parents. They still need time together.

Allow your in-laws to love you in their own way. If you aren't a hugger but hugging is how they express love, grin and bear it.

If one spouse has a dysfunctional or even dangerous family, it will take time to learn the joy of a healthy family. Don't push.

With a little time and patience, you may soon come to see your in-laws as a second mom and dad. And after all, don't we need all the support we can get?

THOUGHT FOR THE DAY

"If it is possible, as far as it depends on you, live at peace with everyone" (Romans 12:18).

TODAY'S ACTIVITY

Talk with your spouse about what their parents enjoy doing, and plan an event to get to know the parents better. If one set of parents enjoys theater, take them out for an evening. If the others like hunting, borrow some camouflage and spend some time in their element. Or start small with an outing to a special restaurant the couple frequents. Use the event to get to know them better.

Shoulder & Share love. Your spouse is 1 of the greatest gifts God gave your in-laws . . . now they pay forward to you. #bless #honor
@Jennifer_McAfee

SEVENTY-THREE

THE SEX TALK

It's not only okay, but good, to talk about sex.

In a new marriage, it's most likely your initial disagreements will be about one of three things: money, sex, or in-laws. Previous devotions have dealt a bit with money and in-laws, so it's time to address sex.

You each have come into your marriage with different experiences and expectations about sex. The variables are numerous, but include past sexual history, church background, how your parents taught you, exposure to pornography, and self-image and body issues.

If you want to maintain a healthy sex life in your marriage, three things are important. First, understand that God designed sex for marriage. What can feel wrong or dirty outside of marriage helps create intimacy between a husband and wife. Now that you're married, you're free to enjoy sex as God's gift to you.

Second, discuss your doubts and fears. Too many couples are reluctant to talk about this part of their marriage. Be completely open with one another about physical intimacy.

Third, forget everything you see in the movies. Media depictions of sex show picture-perfect, fireworks-in-the-sky moments every time a couple gets together. If that's what you expect, you're going to be disappointed. Learn together and laugh at the embarrassing moments.

If sex becomes a source of conflict in your marriage, don't be afraid to talk to someone about it! Overcome your embarrassment and talk to your pastor or a counselor. Just be sure to consult with someone of the same gender to avoid any hint of temptation. And I know I don't need to tell you this, but have fun as you get to know one another better.

THOUGHT FOR THE DAY

"The husband should fulfill his marital duty to his wife, and likewise the wife to her husband. The wife does not have authority over her own body but yields it to her husband. In the same way, the husband does not have authority over his own body but yields it to his wife" (1 Corinthians 7:3–4).

TODAY'S ACTIVITY

I suspect you're looking forward to today's activity, aren't you? But I hope you didn't miss the point that the physical aspect of sex will be heightened by better understanding and sharing between one another. So do that first. Discuss how your marriage fulfills God's will for you and open up about any questions or fears you may not have expressed so far. And from that point, I'll leave the rest up to you.

Remember that sex is one of the greatest gifts that God given you, keep it sacred, communicate with each other, and have fun!
@pastorjoecyr

SEVENTY-FOUR

EXPOSING SELFISHNESS

Identify and confess any selfish tendencies.

Our society today suffers from an epidemic of selfishness. The average credit card debt in the United States is over $15,000. I realize some people have no other way to deal with unavoidable life emergencies, but in most cases the debt exists because people want what they want, and they want it now.

Spending is just one symptom. Selfishness declares, "I'm number one," in direct contradiction to the central message of the gospel: "others first." A self-centered attitude poisons every area of life: finances, friendships, families, and marriages.

It's easy to fall into the selfishness trap when you forget that everything you have is the result of God's blessing and wonderful provision. How can you tell if you're becoming selfish? Ask yourself these questions:

Do I buy for myself before I give to God and others?

Do I get mad if I don't get credit for something I did?

When things go wrong, is my first response to blame others?

Am I always wanting more and never happy with what I have?

Is there a pattern of broken relationships in my life?

Do I expect others to change for my benefit?

Does being right matter more than making it right?

Do I fail to listen to others because I'm waiting to speak?

Am I a one-upper?

Do I think I deserve better than others?

The more "yes" answers you have, the more you need to search for potential selfish tendencies in your life. If you detect a problem, continue to the next devotion to see what you can do about it.

THOUGHT FOR THE DAY

"Do nothing out of selfish ambition or vain conceit. Rather, in humility value others above yourselves, not looking to your own interests but each of you to the interests of the others" (Philippians 2:3–4).

TODAY'S ACTIVITY

After you answer the questions for yourself, ask your spouse to answer them for you (and to be brutally honest). Perhaps they will see something in you that you haven't detected. Humbly listen to what your spouse says and ask God to make you more aware of any problems you have with selfishness . . . for the good of your marriage.

Giving, not taking, is a vital component in a successful marriage. Give more than you take today to bless your spouse.
@ryandarrow

SEVENTY-FIVE

ELIMINATING SELFISHNESS

Confess and overcome your selfish tendencies.

In the previous devotion we saw that selfishness destroys relationships. Since you're just beginning the most important (human) relationship of your life, you need to uncover and remove any selfish tendencies. The goal for your marriage should be to put your spouse first, and then together to put others first! So if you discover you are selfishly living for yourself, individually or as a couple, here are some ideas for how to become more selfless:

Start tithing. Give the first 10 percent of your income to God. It's one simple and measurable way to put Him first.

Pay for someone else's lunch, with no motive but to bless the person.

Do something for someone anonymously, with no way of taking credit for yourself.

Spend an evening as a couple helping others. Feed the homeless, visit a nursing home or hospital, or babysit for a friend who needs a night out. Don't accept any pay or credit.

Find a regular place to serve. Join a ministry that needs volunteers for thankless jobs (cleaning the bathrooms at church, working in the nursery, etc.).

Budget an amount each month to give to others as God speaks to your heart. Decide together whom you should bless and how.

These are all good ways to reposition a selfish mindset. But before doing anything else, repent and ask God to help you live differently and to recognize dangerous tendencies in the future. The real change must begin in your heart as you make Jesus number one in absolutely every area of your life.

THOUGHT FOR THE DAY

"Who is wise and understanding among you? Let them show it by their good life, by deeds done in the humility that comes from wisdom. But if you harbor bitter envy and selfish ambition in your hearts, do not boast about it or deny the truth" (James 3:13–14).

TODAY'S ACTIVITY

Decide together if and when you would like to commit to one of the suggestions from today's reading, or to create a similar challenge of your own. As you become more attuned to the suffering and needs of people around you, any remnants of selfishness should soon disappear.

Plan family generosity. Commit as a couple to one selfless act a day. Do something for someone else—together.
@randyjumper

SEVENTY-SIX

WATCH AND LEARN

Learn from other people's mistakes.

Wouldn't it be great if you could learn from other people's mistakes instead of insisting on making the same mistakes yourself? I don't understand it, but there's something about human nature that wants to believe I'm an exception. "Heavy drinking has messed other people up, but I can handle it." "Drugs destroy thousands of lives, but I can stop when I want." "I see what happens when people drive recklessly while impaired, but I'm going to take my chances." Why do we think we can take the same course of action and expect different results?

If we could learn from other's mistakes . . .

Addiction would be defeated. We would see the consequences of drugs, alcoholism, and pornography and would never consider such things.

Business failures would be the rare exception. We would witness the unexpected pitfalls of entrepreneurs, and we would avoid them.

Our walk with Jesus would be so much more consistent and strong. After seeing the inevitable results when people drop out of church, listen to ungodly leaders, or make foolish compromises, we wouldn't make the same mistakes.

We would have so many more happy marriages and healthy homes. We would see senseless fights, poor communication, and foolish pride, then we would shudder and determine that would never happen to us.

It's often said that insanity is doing the same thing over and over again but expecting different results. Add a little more sanity to your marriage by learning from the mistakes of others and avoiding the same consequences yourself. You'll be a rare exception, but you won't regret it.

THOUGHT FOR THE DAY

"Out in the open wisdom calls aloud, . . . 'How long will you who are simple love your simple ways? How long will mockers delight in mockery and fools hate knowledge? Repent at my rebuke! Then I will pour out my thoughts to you, I will make known to you my teachings'" (Proverbs 1:20, 22–23).

TODAY'S ACTIVITY

Discuss with your spouse exactly *how* you might learn from the mistakes of others. For example, listen closely whenever older couples talk about their times of struggle; visit long-married couples you know and ask what they would have done differently in their marriage; watch couples who always seem to have problems to detect the source; etc. Create your own plan, then be sure to follow up with it.

Marriage is full of ups and downs. Learn from the success of others, & keep a watchful eye on their failures too.
@MikeBurnette

SEVENTY-SEVEN

ASK YOURSELF . . .

Use a three-question checklist to sustain spiritual growth.

My first book, *Three Questions*, was based on questions found in the book of Galatians. I think they provide a helpful way to keep a clear focus on what is important in marriage.

> Question #1: **"Am I now trying to win the approval of human beings, or of God? Or am I trying to please people? If I were still trying to please people, I would not be a servant of Christ"** (Galatians 1:10).

Are you living to please God or to impress people? When you live to win the approval of people, you fail, because trying to please others is a never-ending quest that ends in disaster. Live to please God instead.

> Question #2: **"Are you so foolish? After beginning by means of the Spirit, are you now trying to finish by means of the flesh?"** (Galatians 3:3)

Early in marriage, you can be overwhelmed by all the emotions—excitement, anxiety, nervousness, fear—and you acknowledge your need for God's strength and direction. But when things start going more smoothly, it's easy to begin relying on yourself. Don't do it! If you do, you're headed for burnout, failure, and disaster.

> Question #3: **"Have I now become your enemy by telling you the truth?"** (Galatians 4:16)

The truth often hurts, but not knowing the truth hurts much, much more. Treasure the people God has put in your life who have your best interests at heart and love you enough to tell you hard truths.

For a healthy marriage, ask yourselves these questions every few months. They will help you stay on track!

THOUGHT FOR THE DAY

"Ask and it will be given to you; seek and you will find; knock and the door will be opened to you. For everyone who asks receives; the one who seeks finds; and to the one who knocks, the door will be opened" (Matthew 7:7–8).

TODAY'S ACTIVITY

Discuss the three questions with your spouse. How do you think they apply to marriage in general? How do you think they apply to *your* marriage?

Marriage is a covenant between three parties. What is your metric that ensures God remains the first party?
@RachelLBRoss

SEVENTY-EIGHT

EARLY RESPONDERS

When it comes to obeying God, sooner is better.

I've stopped making New Year's resolutions. Instead, each year I ask God to reveal a major area of life I need to improve. In 2012, I felt the need to begin obeying God more immediately. I thought my obedience was adequate, but I wanted to be more responsive, to quickly obey without question or doubt. I didn't want to miss special moments or opportunities because of delayed obedience. The results have been really encouraging, and I believe anyone can see similar improvements if they commit to more immediate obedience.

God has a plan for you as a couple, and you can be sure His plan is better than *your* plan! He's involved in your lives, constantly speaking and willing to reveal His plan to you. I challenge you to listen for His voice and immediately respond. The sooner you obey, the clearer you will sense His voice!

When God puts it in your heart to give to someone in need, don't hesitate. When you sense Him telling you to share your faith with a friend or coworker, don't give fear a chance to arise. Instead of worrying what people will think or wondering if something makes sense, obey immediately. God will work through you in remarkable ways!

I urge you to respond more quickly to God and see the results for yourself. If you want some encouragement along the way, I hope you'll check out my book, *Immediate Obedience*. It's filled with fascinating stories of what people experienced after committing to respond to God more quickly. It will help you take a giant step of obedience and faith!

THOUGHT FOR THE DAY

"If anyone obeys his word, love for God is truly made complete in them. This is how we know we are in him: Whoever claims to live in him must live as Jesus did" (1 John 2:5–6).

TODAY'S ACTIVITY

Discuss: What would our marriage be like if we immediately, without hesitation, obeyed God every time He spoke? Pray together and ask God to help you sense and know when He is speaking. Ask Him to help you push past your doubts and fears to immediately say yes to Him. It will be the greatest adventure of your lives!

Instead of filling your minds with reasons not to respond to God, think about the positive reasons for immediate obedience to His voice.
@RyanPMoore

SEVENTY-NINE

IT'S YOUR CHOICE

Choose attitudes that honor God
and strengthen your marriage.

The world is full of all kinds of people. Below is a list Cindy and I made of who we don't—and do—want to be.

Whiners are always looking for attention and always complaining about the attention they don't receive. Be a **winner**, instead. Always look for an opportunity to grow, improve, and make a difference.

Critics can find fault with everything. They dwell more on small disappointments than major positive events. They can always tell you what to do but are rarely willing to actually help. Be an **encourager** instead. Praise strengths and celebrate successes.

Cynics believe everyone is out for themselves and that no one tells the whole truth. Be an **optimist** instead. Give others the benefit of the doubt and find good in every person.

Misers are ultra-selfish, obsessed with accumulating wealth, but not for sharing. These "miser-able" people never experience the true joy of giving. Be a **giver** instead—of time, resources, love, energy, and money.

Know-It-Alls assume they're wise and everyone else is stupid. They have a unique way of putting you down and making you feel inferior. Be a **learner** instead. Always seek additional knowledge and personal growth.

Gossips delight in sharing "juicy" information about others. They have no authentic relationships because no one trusts them to keep confidences. Be a loyal **friend**, instead. Be a person who can be trusted with sensitive information and genuinely wants to help.

Be aware of bad attitudes so you can avoid them. You choose (and can change) your attitudes and personality, and your choices will affect not only your marriage, but your entire life. Examine yourself closely . . . and choose wisely.

THOUGHT FOR THE DAY

"Finally, brothers and sisters, whatever is true, whatever is noble, whatever is right, whatever is pure, whatever is lovely, whatever is admirable—if anything is excellent or praiseworthy—think about such things" (Philippians 4:8).

TODAY'S ACTIVITY

With your spouse, review the list of both the negative and positive attitudes/personalities. As you do, try to identify people you know who fit the description. Make a note of those who set consistent positive examples and be sure to let them know the next time you see them. Spend time in prayer, asking God to remove any negative attitudes and replace them with fresh new positive ones that honor Him in everything you do.

Your attitude determines the direction of your marriage. Consider: "What's it like to be married to me?"
@Aaron_Hlavin

EIGHTY

WHEN SURPRISES AREN'T

Make plans, but learn to cope with unanticipated surprises.

In preparation for our twenty-fifth anniversary, I started setting aside money three years in advance so I could pay cash to buy Cindy a new wedding ring. I was so careful to keep it a secret. Just a few days before I would finally get to see the culmination of my three-year plan, Cindy and I were both in the bathroom getting ready. I noticed a voicemail on my phone, hit the speaker button, and punched up the volume. Cindy and I both heard the message clearly: "Rod, your ring is ready."

The surprise wasn't a surprise anymore. I said, "Well, guess I might as well go get the ring." I got in my truck and started crying as I drove to the jewelry store. Thirty minutes later, I got back and said, "Here's your ring. Happy anniversary." My grand plan had fallen flat, but Cindy loved the ring and didn't care that it wasn't a well-orchestrated surprise.

Plans don't always work out. Things go wrong. Accidents happen. Emergencies arise. Surprises aren't. I've seen so many couples disappointed when carefully thought out plans didn't materialize—often over the tiniest issues.

It's good to dream and plan, whether or not those things happen on your timetable. Make plans, but expect the unexpected. Trust that God not only knows what you need, but when you need it. Sustained faith will help you thrive in spite of postponed vacations, surprise pregnancies, missed flights, and even spoiled anniversary surprises!

THOUGHT FOR THE DAY

"In their hearts humans plan their course, but the LORD establishes their steps" (Proverbs 16:9).

TODAY'S ACTIVITY

Sit down with your spouse and discuss: What are the most important plans we have for the future? How important is it that those plans go just as we anticipate? What will we do if they don't materialize as we hope? Do we have enough trust in God to get us through any and every unexpected detour and problem we will encounter? If not, what do we need to do?

Be ready for roller-coaster living in the game called life. Strategize & dream together but know you can't plan everything.
@andrewtempleton

EIGHTY-ONE

PEACE SIGNS

Peace is the antidote to conflict, anxiety, and stress.

It seems that people talk about peace all the time. We see traditional peace signs, bumper sticker reminders to "Pray for peace," and organized marches. But what, exactly, *is* peace? What does it look like in a home? Below are some signs of what peace is—and isn't.

Peace *is*:

An inner feeling of calm, knowing that in spite of the turmoil around you, everything is going to be okay.

The absence of internal anxiety and pressure.

A quiet confidence that exists even when there is no outward explanation for it.

Knowing you aren't alone and don't have to handle the stress of life by yourself, because God is working on your behalf.

A byproduct of prayer. As you draw close to God, you can experience a sense of peace that's beyond human explanation or understanding.

Peace *isn't*:

Having everything go just right. You can have peace in the middle of your worst circumstances and your biggest storms.

The absence of noise. Our home is peaceful, but it's anything but quiet! One night I counted six simultaneous conversations going on (plus a barking dog), yet it was still wonderfully peaceful.

The absence of conflict. I know some homes where couples don't even communicate enough to disagree. That's not peace; it's avoidance!

Peace results from transferring your worries, anxieties, and fear to Jesus through prayer and worship. In a marriage, peace includes the confident assurance husband and wife are together forever, filled with love and forgiveness and determined to be lifelong followers of Jesus. Doesn't that sound wonderful? I pray that your marriage and home are always filled with peace.

THOUGHT FOR THE DAY

"Do not be anxious about anything, but in every situation, by prayer and petition, with thanksgiving, present your requests to God. And the peace of God, which transcends all understanding, will guard your hearts and your minds in Christ Jesus" (Philippians 4:6–7).

TODAY'S ACTIVITY

Complete the following sentence in regard to your spouse: "Lately you haven't seemed to be at peace about . . ." See if your spouse agrees with your observation. Act as one another's counselor and offer your best advice, including how the other spouse might transfer more of their anxiety to Jesus in order to experience a much-needed sense of peace.

Pray with your spouse and drink deeply of the peace that comes from including God in your shared past, present, and future.
@NathanKollar

EIGHTY-TWO

CHAIR AND CHAIR ALIKE

Tolerate (even enjoy) gender differences.

Have you ever noticed the differences between a woman's chair and a man's chair? A woman's chair must look good; a man's chair must feel good. A woman's chair is covered with pillows; a man's chair is covered with remote controls, cookie crumbs, and Dr. Pepper stains. A woman's chair enables you to sit up and maintain good posture; a man's chair flops back so he can put his feet up and forget about the day's problems. A woman can sit in another chair; a man has *his* chair—and you'd better not sit in it!

That's just a chair we're talking about. I could expound on communication, memory, emotion, and more. But let's just agree that major differences between men and women exist and decide what to do about them. Here are helpful things to remember as you negotiate learning to relate to each other as a man and a woman:

Neither one of you is right or wrong, so acknowledge and discuss your differences. Be honest about what you're like and what you prefer.

Compromise. If you don't like sharing details and (s)he wants all the details, meet in the middle. If (s)he doesn't like to talk when (s)he gets home, wait a few minutes before asking.

Be patient. It'll take time to become accustomed to your conversational rhythms. Eventually you'll be like the old people who finish each other's sentences.

Laugh at yourself. Soon you'll both be laughing.

Maybe you can come by our house sometime to discuss these things. If you do, just don't sit in my chair!

THOUGHT FOR THE DAY

"Each one of you also must love his wife as he loves himself, and the wife must respect her husband" (Ephesians 5:33).

TODAY'S ACTIVITY

Each of you can choose a different area where men and women are quite different and list the differences (using the "chair" example as a guide, if you want). Have some fun with this exercise, but you'll probably see clearly a lot of truth as you read your examples to one another. Agree to let each other be the unique (if not peculiar) person God created you to be.

Differences are the spice of life! Discover, respect, and celebrate who your spouse is without assumption.
@Jennifer_McAfee

EIGHTY-THREE

REGRETS, I'VE HAD A FEW

Start now to minimize regrets.

I try not to regret things in the past because I can't change them. But when it comes to my marriage, I wish I had done a few things differently when Cindy and I started out twenty-seven years ago. I share them with you because I would love to help you avoid the same mistakes.

> **I wish I had established a yearly marriage checkup with a pastor or counselor. It would have been especially helpful early in marriage to talk through little things so they couldn't become bigger things.**

> **When we first got married, Cindy and I went to dinner every month with friends to one of the top restaurants in our city. But as life got busier with work and family demands, we stopped our monthly outings. If we hadn't, our friendships would be deeper.**

> **I used sarcasm way too much in trying to be funny—a habit I developed in junior high. Cindy didn't deserve my ill-advised putdowns. If I could start over, I would treat her with the honor she deserves as my cherished wife.**

> **I worried too much about things that don't matter. If I had learned sooner from Cindy's easygoing demeanor, our marriage would have had much less stress.**

> **I wish we had established a regular prayer time together from the beginning, even though we both worked two jobs. I've learned that life will never be less busy, but prayer helps put all that busyness into perspective!**

You won't avoid making mistakes, no matter how hard you try. But now you don't have to make the same ones I did!

THOUGHT FOR THE DAY

"Do not conform to the pattern of this world, but be transformed by the renewing of your mind. Then you will be able to test and approve what God's will is—his good, pleasing and perfect will" (Romans 12:2).

TODAY'S ACTIVITY

Discuss with your spouse: Do you see us doing anything on this list that we're likely to regret later? Are we doing (or have we done) anything so far in our marriage that's likely to be regrettable someday. If so, what should we do about it?

The greatest way to avoid regrets in your marriage is to openly communicate and receive constructive feedback.
@pastorjoecyr

EIGHTY-FOUR

CLOSE TO THE TRUTH

Dare to let your spouse make you a better person.

Cindy and I had only been married a couple years when we moved to Fargo, North Dakota. We served a wonderful church there, working with a pastor who was a life mentor for me. My area of ministry experienced phenomenal growth. The people were warm, loving, and caring. So I was stunned one winter evening when Cindy suddenly declared, "It's time for us to leave here." I asked, "What are you talking about? Things are going great. We're loved. The ministry is growing." She replied, "That's all true, but you've quit growing as a leader and a person. It's time for a change."

My first instinct was to argue, but as I thought about it, I realized she was right. My success was a blind spot that kept me from seeing I was stagnant. It wasn't easy to hear, but I needed to hear it from someone who loved me enough to share a difficult truth.

You need someone who loves you enough to help you grow, to point out things you can't see. Spiritual growth sometimes requires facing hard truths and making difficult changes, and a loving spouse who will help you face that truth is indispensable.

Too many people are enablers, telling a spouse what (s)he wants to hear. Even if the intentions are good, enablers short-circuit the growth process. Don't be an enabler! Love your spouse enough to declare truth no one else is willing to share. Say it gently, in love, and at the proper time, but say it!

You won't be sorry. A few months after her bold statement, Cindy and I moved to North Little Rock, Arkansas. I'm still serving in the same church twenty-two years later . . . and hopefully still growing!

THOUGHT FOR THE DAY

"Buy the truth and do not sell it—wisdom, instruction and insight as well" (Proverbs 23:23).

TODAY'S ACTIVITY

It's still early in your marriage, but you've been together long enough to ask some hard questions. Ask one another: Do you think I enable you in any way? Is there something you've been wanting to tell me, but are holding back for some reason? What do you think I need to do to become a better person? Etc.

Lies are powerful. Keep your marriage honest by prioritizing truth-telling in your home. Be kind but be open and genuine.
@ryandarrow

EIGHTY-FIVE

PUT A SUNSET ON YOUR SORROW

Set a deadline for dealing with disappointment.

Cindy and I were anticipating a much-needed vacation to Palm Springs, California. We spent months in advance making plans, arranging tickets, and reading up on restaurants we wanted to try. The day before we were scheduled to leave, I got a call telling me one of the pillars of our church—who was also a dear friend—had passed away. I called Cindy to tell her, and she said, "I guess we aren't going to Palm Springs anymore." I said, "No. I don't think so." I called the airline and canceled our trip.

Were we disappointed? Certainly! Yet we knew our canceled vacation was trivial compared to the loss to our church, and to the man's family. It wasn't the first time our plans were changed because of a crisis, and it won't be the last.

We've learned a technique for dealing with disappointment: we put a sunset on our sorrow. We allow a short time to grieve and then move on. The longest time we've ever allotted was three days—and that was too long!

Instead of a vacation, Cindy and I joined others for a beautiful remembrance of our dear friend and had a nice dinner together that evening. It wasn't what we had planned, but we still have fond memories of that day.

Unexpected events change plans. Trips get cancelled. But don't be disappointed indefinitely! It might ruin a day, but don't let it ruin any more than that. Instead, move on to find fresh joy and new happiness.

THOUGHT FOR THE DAY

"We also glory in our sufferings, because we know that suffering produces perseverance; perseverance, character; and character, hope" (Romans 5:3–4).

TODAY'S ACTIVITY

Individually, think back to a time when some of your big plans were canceled. What were the circumstances? What was your immediate response? How long were you disappointed? Share your story with your spouse and then come to some agreement on how you'll try to respond the next time the two of you face a major disappointment together.

Don't dwell on disappointments; grieve appropriately, and then move on. Set an alarm and wake up! Joy comes in the morning.
@randyjumper

EIGHTY-SIX

SAY IT TODAY

Don't wait for crisis situations to express your love.

Several years ago my friend Glenn was diagnosed with cancer in his kidney. He and his wife, Reta, had lived a good life. They had a newly married son and were looking forward to being grandparents one day. But with one statement from a doctor, their lives changed. Suddenly, everything they had planned and hoped for seemed uncertain. Thankfully, Glenn's surgery was successful and he has been cancer free for eight years. But the lessons Glenn and Reta learned during the cancer battle are still with them.

In fact, Reta wrote letters to Glenn and me. She wondered if she had been expressive enough about the extent of her love for him, so she gave him a long, detailed letter that he still cherishes. And she told me that she is much more grateful for each new day now that she has seen that life is so uncertain. She's trying to get better at telling people how much they mean to her—and not just on holidays, birthdays, and other "expected" times.

I urge you to take Reta's advice. Hug each other every chance you get. Say, "I love you" ten times a day. Find creative ways to express your love to each other. Don't ever take it for granted. Don't wait until cancer or a life-altering crisis to tell your spouse how much (s)he means to you. Early in the morning, when you wake and your spouse is still sleeping, thank God for another day together. The day will come when you won't have tomorrow to do it.

THOUGHT FOR THE DAY

"I thank my God every time I remember you. In all my prayers for all of you, I always pray with joy because of your partnership in the gospel from the first day until now, being confident in this, that he who began a good work in you will carry it on to completion until the day of Christ Jesus" (Philippians 1:3–6).

TODAY'S ACTIVITY

Take time today to document your love. Write a detailed and specific letter that spells out all the things you admire about your spouse and everything you're thankful for. You may be taking each other's love for granted now, but put aside the letter you receive. You'll treasure those written words forever.

Communicating your feelings regularly will keep your spouse informed and your heart conformed to your spouse.
@MikeBurnette

EIGHTY-SEVEN

A MATTER OF TIMING

Trust God when you don't see results,
and keep doing good in the meantime.

Years ago I had the first PC at our church. It was rocket fast—a 386.25 megahertz with a whopping four megabytes of RAM. I could go on the Internet and download a webpage in less than a minute! Today if I see the hourglass and have to wait a couple of seconds, I'm ready to upgrade.

Most people are obsessed with speed, and incredibly impatient. At red lights we try to predict which lane will move faster. At the grocery store we scan the number of items in baskets or look for someone with a dreaded checkbook to avoid getting in a slow line. We want what we want, and we want it now!

Unfortunately, we tend to take that same mindset into our relationships with God. We want to trust God and follow His principles—in marriage, finances, and behavior. We start with the best of intentions, but then we get impatient. We don't want to wait. Our impatience is at the core of most of our issues with God. When we pray for something and don't see results right away, we want to know, "Where is my healing?" "Why isn't God answering my prayers?" "If this tithing thing really works, it had better happen this week!"

Trusting God is a huge step of faith. Trusting His timing is even more difficult. But you can be sure God knows what He is doing. Keep growing in your faith, continue to do good, and leave the timing to Him. He is working to orchestrate His plan for you and for others around you to achieve incredible results . . . at just the right time.

THOUGHT FOR THE DAY

"Let us not become weary in doing good, for at the proper time we will reap a harvest if we do not give up" (Galatians 6:9).

TODAY'S ACTIVITY

Have a Bible study with your spouse tonight. Read and discuss Exodus 32—the account of the golden calf. Look specifically for the numerous consequences that resulted because of the people's impatience. Then spend a little time comparing the Israelite society to your own. Do you see any similarities?

Situations that require patience can grow hope in you or resentment. Choose which one you want to live with in the end.
@RachelLBRoss

EIGHTY-EIGHT

LOSE SOME UNWANTED WEIGHT

Grudges get far too heavy if you don't let them go.

Cindy and I have never had a lot of tension in our marriage, but one time she shared something she shouldn't have, which cost me credibility in an important relationship. I was embarrassed and frustrated. She was tearful and apologetic, and she asked my forgiveness.

I *said* I forgave her, but in reality I carried that offense around for days. I didn't yell or vent, but I was withdrawn and quieter than usual. She could tell the difference.

I was holding on to a grudge. The dictionary defines a *grudge* as a "feeling of ill will or resentment." A grudge is a burden that weighs you down, stops your progress, and keeps you frozen in place. It locks you in a cycle of bitterness, anger, hurt, and regret that affects every part of your life, including your marriage. When you refuse to let it go, it becomes impossible to forgive.

I'm ashamed to admit it, but ten days later I was still holding that grudge. We were taking communion at church, but I felt heavy and distracted. While everyone was worshiping, I knelt and began to weep. Cindy knelt beside me, put her arm around me, and started praying. I choked out: "I'm so sorry. Please forgive me for holding on to this. I have to let this go." We cried together, but immediately it felt like a thousand-pound weight had been lifted off my back.

So don't just forgive; forgive *quickly*. Don't hold a grudge. The moment you let it go and forgive the offense you'll feel so much better!

THOUGHT FOR THE DAY

"Bear with each other and forgive one another if any of you has a grievance against someone. Forgive as the Lord forgave you" (Colossians 3:13).

TODAY'S ACTIVITY

If you're holding on to a hurt, confess it to your spouse. Let it go right now! Ask for forgiveness. Cry together, pray together, and move forward. And if neither of you has a grudge against the other, consider if there might be someone else you feel resentment toward. Grudges are insidious. Even eliminating grudges toward *other* people can strengthen your marriage.

Marriage is a platform to put the gospel on display. The choice to forgive is an opportunity to demonstrate God's character.
@RyanPMoore

EIGHTY-NINE

WISHING TOO LATE

Don't waste time wishing; spend your time doing.

I don't know much about farming, but I've learned important principles from my farmer friends. Liz Bevis told me: **"**A seed is sealed. Only when it's put in its designated place, the ground, can it bring forth fruit. If you leave it in the barn it's still seed, and a hundred years later it'll still be seed."

When it comes to your marriage and family, it's not enough to know what you want to do. You have to actually plant the right seeds to prepare for the desired harvest.

I hear any number of " wishes" from people late in life. For example:

I wish I had made my marriage a bigger priority.

I wish I had spent less time at work.

I wish I hadn't put money before my marriage.

I wish I had led my family in devotions and prayer.

I wish I had told my spouse "I love you" and "I'm sorry" more often.

I wish I hadn't insisted on my own way so often.

I wish I had taught my family the importance of sacrifice.

I wish I had slowed down more.

I wish I hadn't yelled as much.

I wish I had bought more flowers.

I wish I had spent less time [hunting/golfing/shopping/etc.] and more time at home.

These "wishes" are like unplanted seeds. They had potential but couldn't do any good sitting dormant in the barn. It's still early for you, so plant the seeds you desire for your marriage and family *now*!

THOUGHT FOR THE DAY

"Those who sow with tears will reap with songs of joy. Those who go out weeping, carrying seed to sow, will return with songs of joy, carrying sheaves with them" (Psalm 126:5–6).

TODAY'S ACTIVITY

Now that you're at least several months into your marriage, discuss the busyness that has probably crept into your lives. How can you keep it under control? Determine the best days and times to reserve for one another when you can plant the seeds you want to grow in your marriage and in your family. It's crucial not to start making excuses at this point, or you're likely to join those with a remorseful "wish" list later in life.

Don't miss out on your future by neglecting your present.
@Aaron_Hlavin

NINETY

JUST A REMINDER.

Hold fast to some no-matter-what rules and goals.

Marriage is a constantly evolving relationship. You will change. Your spouse will change. Your life will take unexpected turns. Responsibilities will shift. Each year will bring new challenges and fresh opportunities. So as you make the transition from "after the honeymoon" into the fullness of married life, I want to leave you with a few simple reminders.

Never stop asking questions.

Never stop learning.

Never stop growing.

Never stop changing.

Say "I love you" every day.

Hug often.

Look for and find the best in each other.

Be outrageously generous.

Practice immediate obedience.

Share sorrows.

Celebrate victories and successes.

Invest in others.

Thank God often.

Create an intentional lasting legacy.

Commit to growing old together.

Serve Jesus until He returns, or until you enter His presence, to be together with Him for all eternity.

I pray that God will use you together in a greater way than He could ever use you apart. May your lives be filled with the joy of His presence as you faithfully serve Him individually and as a couple.

THOUGHT FOR THE DAY

"Blessed is the one . . . whose delight is in the law of the Lord, and who meditates on his law day and night. That person is like a tree planted by streams of water, which yields its fruit in season and whose leaf does not wither—whatever they do prospers" (Psalm 1:1–3).

TODAY'S ACTIVITY

You've done it a few times already, but once again sit down and make a list of the things you like about your spouse. (And then let it become a regular habit.) As with each time before, add some new specific things you haven't included previously. Then go out and model a vibrant, godly marriage to everyone you come into contact with.

Create healthy habits & enjoy the journey.
Your spouse is a gift from God; treasure the
gift & remain best friends for life.
@andrewtempleton

AFTERWORDS

FROM TYLER:

Before we got married, people told me marriage was tough. At times it actually got me down. I didn't want to fight or have problems; I just wanted our marriage to be perfect even though I knew we would never be perfect.

In the days leading up to our wedding, I began thinking about and trying to prepare myself for the challenges of marriage. Then my dad started writing his marriage thoughts to Emilie and me. It was something I looked forward to each day. I couldn't wait to get the Facebook notification that I was tagged in a status from my dad. Emilie and I would sit down, read the status together, dig through it, and see how it applied to us.

I remember one day we were facing a big problem. We didn't know what to do about it. Just as we were sitting down to talk it out, both of our phones beeped with the notification of my dad's post. I believe without a doubt that God was directing my dad's thoughts, because his marriage advice was dead-on about what we were facing. It made the next couple of minutes so much easier.

I don't know what problems other people will face in marriage, but what I do know is my dad's advice applied to *my* marriage. I know that some of it helped us avoid future problems, and some of it addressed a problem at just the right moment.

Before my wedding day I felt stressed and nervous about the problems we might face, but after my dad's advice I feel prepared to face any situation. I appreciate someone who has gone through the journey openly sharing what he experienced so that we could be better prepared.

FROM EMILIE:

Having been married a few short, amazingly wonderful months, I'm so grateful for the wisdom Tyler and I received from this book. I strongly believe that it helped us navigate the beginning of our marriage much more successfully than we would have otherwise! It equipped us to deal with situations we have already faced and showed us areas of potential struggle that we need to guard against.

This book not only helped prepare us for marriage by providing wonderful advice, it also helped us start conversations about the strengths and weaknesses that are present in every marriage. It got us talking about how we handle conflict, finances, relationships, and expectations. Instead of waiting for problems to occur and then discussing these topics, we were able to talk about them in a non-emotionally charged setting and lay the foundation for a strong marriage.

As I read these daily devotions, my reactions were varied. Some days I would read the advice and think to myself, *Well, that's obvious. Of course that's what we should do!* But as Tyler and I settled into our routine as a married couple, I realized that when you're in the middle of an argument or a stressful situation, it's not always intuitive or easy to follow the advice that seemed so clear. However, reading the devotions beforehand helped prepare us for situations like those, and many times I would be reminded of a phrase or story from this book that helped me regain perspective.

Several times the daily devotion would come right before or right after we dealt with a situation concerning that exact same topic. I remember at least two days on our honeymoon alone just laughing at how spot-on the subject for the day was! The topics are so relevant and true!

Other times the devotion contained good, trustworthy advice that I knew we would revisit often in our marriage—solid principles that would help us make and keep our marriage strong. I firmly believe that these are devotions that should not only be read once during your first ninety days of marriage; they should be revisited often.

As I've gone back and reread the advice, I've found many topics I thought would be a nonissue that instead are very real and present in our young marriage as we learn how to live and make decisions together. As our marriage grows, as we learn how to be the husband and wife each other needs, different strengths and weaknesses become clear. Going through these devotions the first time helped lay a foundation that greatly helped us during our first months of marriage, and I have no doubt they will continue to serve the same purpose as we grow together.

These devotions are great conversation starters, great thought-provokers, great incentives to truly examine the way we deal with relationships, finances, and conflict. They have helped Tyler and me so much in our first months together, and have strengthened our marriage and our love. These first months of marriage have been the best of my life, and I'm so excited to keep growing with the husband I love more every day in a marriage we are determined to keep strong!

90 DATES FOR $10 DOLLARS OR LESS

(Many thanks to the numerous people
who contributed ideas for this list.)

1. Find a beautiful spot surrounded by nature, pull out a blanket, and drink sparkling grape juice in fancy glasses.

2. Have coffee at a local bookstore and read/discuss a good book.

3. Buy some ice cream to eat as you walk around a park.

4. Volunteer at a local food bank (or similar charity) together.

5. Buy and play a new board game (and start a collection for future evenings).

6. Take the dogs to the park, then get them a new toy at the pet store.

7. Have a photo scavenger hunt. Leave home with a list of random goofy things to search for. Take pictures as you find them around town.

8. Picnic near a lake.

9. Tour various local museums. (Most are free.)

10. Prune weeds in a community garden.

11. Find some recipes that look intriguing, buy the ingredients, then return home and make something new together (cupcakes, homemade egg rolls, or whatever you like). Veg out on the couch watching a movie and eating the goodies you made.

12. Recall good memories by playing "Where am I?" One person describes a place familiar to the other (a previous vacation spot, a Bed and Breakfast, a favorite restaurant, etc.). The other one tries to guess.

13. Go geocaching. All that's needed is a car and a smartphone app.

14. Enjoy free movies in the park.

15. Sit and talk in the lobby of a posh hotel.

16. Check out a greenway or walking trail you haven't tried yet.

17. Disc golf is free, but you might need to borrow some discs.

18. Sit on the patio and look through old photos.

19. Go hiking together. You get to enjoy each other's company and God's lovely creation. Use the ten dollars for salve and bandages for your blisters.

20. Have a duct tape night. Each person gets a roll of duct tape and has to make something for the other.

21. Take a boat ride at sunset.

22. Go four-wheeling.

23. Do some target shooting.

24. Go fishing. (Look for "free days" when you don't need a license.)

25. Go shopping to pick a specific and/or extravagant gift you *would* buy for your spouse if you had unlimited cash to spend.

26. Have a talk-about-our-future date. It doesn't cost anything to dream for hours and hours.

27. Go to a bookstore and take fifteen minutes to select three books or book titles that best describe your spouse.

28. While your spouse is away, convert your home into a relaxing (and romantic) spa as a surprise.

29. Go to open houses and dream together about what type of home you hope to buy someday.

30. Go to a mall and watch people. Spend the ten dollars at the food court.

31. Park near an airport where you can watch all the planes coming and going.

32. Walk around the outside perimeter of a golf course and see who can find the most rogue golf balls.

33. Compile a list of the top ten movies you would both like to see together and begin to collect them as they go on sale. On date night when you can't go out, pull one off the shelf and you're ready to go.

34. Fly kites. Better yet, make your own kites and go fly them.

35. Hunt deer using a couple's stand instead of a climber/single-seater stand. Share stories and create games to pass the time. The breathtaking sunrises and sunsets provide some romantic moments to share with your love.

36. Eat dinner at home, and then go out to share a dessert at a fancy restaurant.

37. Have a no-drive drive-in movie! Cuddle in the backyard or on a rooftop with some popcorn and hot chocolate while you watch a movie on your laptop.

38. Take a trolley ride, browse at some new places, and stop for gourmet coffee.

39. Shoot some pool.

40. Pack up pizza, hot chocolate, cookies, blankets, and coats, and get away from city lights to stargaze on a clear winter night. Even better, wait for announcements of meteor showers.

41. Make a run to a favorite drive-in ice cream place on a hot Saturday afternoon.

42. Go bowling.

43. Go bicycle riding to a favorite romantic spot.

44. Share an appetizer at a local restaurant that airs a sports event you both want to see (football, basketball, hockey, or whatever).

45. Walk around downtown to window shop or go to antique stores.

46. Compile a list of the days and times for local restaurant two-for-one specials or other bargains. On days when you've both been too busy to fix dinner, go out to eat and just catch up with one another.

47. Visit an art gallery or watch for affordable art walks.

48. Have hot chocolate on the roof at dusk as the city lights begin to sparkle.

49. Picnic in front of the fireplace and make s'mores—it's cozy and bug free.

50. Revisit a location that was significant to you while you were dating or early in your marriage. You need not spend money this time, but relive the memories from that place.

51. Play mini golf, and enjoy competing with one another.

52. Go roller-skating. Watch for coupons for free admission so all you have to pay for is skate rental.

53. Every once in a while, walk around the neighborhood together. Note the change of seasons, homes bought and sold, and other signs of time passing.

54. Write a message about how special your spouse is and send it off into the unknown (via helium balloon, bottle released in the ocean, etc.) with a request for the finder to notify you.

55. Plant tulip or daffodil bulbs together in the fall and photograph your flowers in spring.

56. Take a photo in the same location with the same pose on the same day each month or year. Start a collection.

57. Each spouse should list four or five things he or she might buy at the dollar store. (Don't show your lists to one another.) Then go to the store with five dollars each and purchase what you believe is on the other's list. Meet afterward and see who came closest to matching the spouse's list.

58. Use an evening to catch up with old friends you haven't seen or heard from in a while. Call or Skype them, see what they're up to, and let them know how great your marriage is going.

59. Learn how to fold a newspaper into a boat. Have boat races on a local pond, lake, or fountain. The winner buys ice cream to console the one who comes in second.

60. Send your spouse a text message to go to a particular location. Meet him or her there with a favorite dessert.

61. Wash the car with a water balloon war.

62. Make breakfast at midnight.

63. Buy matching crazy socks and *wear* them. It can be your secret smile.

64. Go for a walk in the rain. Leave the umbrella at home.

65. Buy a suet cake (about a dollar) and place it outside a window in your kitchen area. Wait for brightly colored birds (blue jays, cardinals, etc.) to show up, and photograph them.

66. Spend an evening at the local library.

67. Spend the ten dollars on gas, then drive around while you listen to music and talk.

68. Work on your swing at the batting cages.

69. Go to a large garage sale or flea market with five dollars each and a category to shop for (most beautiful, most bizarre, largest, etc.). Set a time limit and place to meet, and see who makes the better purchases.

70. Spend an entire evening (or day) together doing one spouse's favorite hobby. It might be videogames, scrapbooking, gardening, or whatever. The sacrifice of the other spouse makes those days true bonding experiences.

71. Community (or even high school) plays are inexpensive and can be surprisingly good.

72. Buy twenty rolls of pennies, go to a local fountain, and make up games to play with your 1,000 pennies (aim for the statue, try for closest to a specific target, etc.). When kids start to gather, you have plenty of pennies to share with them. (And often the money is collected for a good cause.)

73. Play Bingo with senior citizens. Make friends with someone who needs one.

74. Go to a high school football game to support the team, or a peewee soccer game to have some laughs.

75. Most cities have free music going on *somewhere*, whether concerts in the park, bookstores, restaurants, etc.

76. Watch for free community events: cooking classes, dance lessons, pottery, etc.

77. Take a walk on the beach, or walk beside a nearby river or lake and pretend it's a beach getaway.

78. Spend an evening at Ikea, Costco, Sam's Club, or other warehouse to get ideas for one another's preferences for what you might buy when you do have the opportunity.

79. Recreate your first date as closely as possible.

80. Plan your twenty-fifth wedding anniversary. Start with your top ten desired locations, and narrow it down to one or two options. Use the ten dollars to start a savings account for that special trip.

81. Take turns choosing videos to watch on YouTube.

82. Go to an art supply store and see what you can create for your home for ten dollars.

83. Spend the ten dollars to buy your favorite songs on iTunes, and then make a playlist of "your" songs.

84. Think of elderly (or otherwise needy) people you know about from friends or church. Spend an evening together helping someone who really needs it (doing chores, spending time, helping with shopping, etc.).

85. Conduct your own version of the Food Network program, *Chopped*. Grab four unrelated items from your pantry/fridge and create a meal.

86. Have a "team" dinner. Invite four couples over. One brings appetizer, one brings salad, one brings dessert, one brings side dishes, and you provide the entrée. Everyone spends under ten dollars, and you get a great meal and good companionship. (Or make it a progressive dinner where you travel to each couple's home for that particular course.)

87. List a few people who've been supportive and helpful to you in your marriage so far. Write thank-you letters and/or make nice cards, but write and deliver them anonymously. Give the people a few days to wonder who appreciates them so much before you tell them in person.

88. Go to a children's park after dark, when you have it to yourselves. Sit in the swings and enjoy the evening together.

89. Go to a large store and play "The Price Is Right." Choose an item at a distance, guess the price, and see who comes closer.

90. Stay home, light some candles, put on some music, and turn in early.

ABOUT ROD LOY

Rod Loy has been in full-time pastoral ministry for twenty-nine years. He is currently senior pastor at First Assembly of God in North Little Rock, Arkansas, a 102 year-old church. In the last thirteen years, under Rod's leadership, the church has grown to over 4,400 in average weekly attendance on six campuses.

His passion for missions has taken him to forty different countries. First Assembly gives over a million dollars to missions every year and has helped to plant more than 1,100 churches in sixty-three nations.

He is the author of *3 Questions: A Powerful Grid to Help You Live by the Grace of God* and *Immediate Obedience: The Adventure of Tuning In to God.*

Rod's unique approach to leadership has led him to adventures in the "Real World," including working as a volunteer lifeguard at a water park. A former children's pastor, Rod has helped develop the Faith Case curriculum for children and is still actively involved with kids. In fact, his office is in the preschool department!

He and his wife, Cindy, have been married for twenty-seven years and have two sons, Tyler and Parker, and a daughter-in-law, Emilie. The whole family enjoys cheering for the Dallas Mavericks, four-wheeling, and the Arkansas Razorbacks.

The Loys live in North Little Rock, Arkansas.

For more information about First Assembly, ministry resources,
or to watch services online, go to **firstnlr.com**.

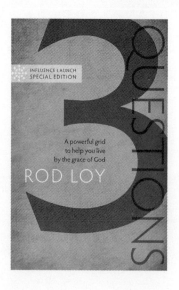
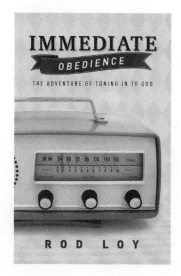